BULLETPROOF HOMEWORK PLANNER

NAME:

PHONE NUMBER:

SEMESTER:

ISBN: 9781726656269

Introduction

Welcome to a easier way of managing homework and projects. The Bulletproof Planner is designed not just to help you get an iron-clad grip on all of your work for this semester, but also to help you start honing the organizational and motivational skills that will make you successful in life.

The truth is, unless you want to be a doctor, no one will care how much chemistry or biology you remember in 20 years. You can be super successful in life without being particularly successful in geometry or European history. **But it's very hard to be successful in life if you don't get your work done.** There are plenty of high achieving successful adults who don't remember anything about chemistry, but there aren't many high achieving successful adults who don't put in the effort, or who forget to do their work, or who do it but fail to turn it in.

This planner is for high potential people who are held back by "executive function" challenges. Like a Ferrari with a flat tire, you just have an issue that's getting in the way of demonstrating your true potential. Maybe you are forgetful or disorganized, or you procrastinate, or you're just anxious and overwhelmed by what seems like a mountain of work. The Bulletproof Planner will help you build some solid skills to solve your problem. The only hitch is, you have to use it. It's simple, but it takes a commitment on your part to do it. Follow the simple instructions, one day at a time, and you will become bulletproof!

What's inside:

Monthly Calendar Pages
Don't let long term assignments sneak up on you the night before they are due.

Daily Homework Pages
This is where the rubber meets the road every day. Capture and manage your homework using the planner, and improve your life by eliminating the procrastination and anguish caused by an untamed out-of-control homework mess.

With the Bulletproof Planner you will start by mastering the homework beast and go on to truly own the executive skills that will make you successful in anything you do.

BULLETPROOF YOUR HOMEWORK IN 7 STEPS

1. **Capture it!** Write your homework in the daily planner box for each class, **<u>before you leave class</u>**.
    *   Check the board
    *   Ask the teacher
    *   Ask a classmate
    *   **Don't leave the room without it!**

1. When you start your homework, start by getting organized.
    *   Look over your captured homework assignments
    *   When is it due?
    *   How high a priority is it? (1 = High, 3 = Low)
    *   How much time do you estimate it will take?
    *   Is there anything you need to complete your homework, or any help you need? If so, write that in the "Help!" box at the bottom.

2. In the "Heads Up!" box, note any projects or tests with dates further in the future that you need to keep track of.
    *   Write the future due date on the Monthly Calendar page.
    *   Take a minute to look over the assignment to make a realistic estimate of how much work will be required. This is crucial; don't leave it until the night before.
    *   Based on your estimate of the work that will be required for the project, plan backwards from the due date to set some key milestones along the way, so you won't be overwhelmed by a tsunami of work at the end. Write your milestone dates on the Monthly Calendar.

3. Check the Monthly Calendar for any dates or milestones that are due tomorrow or very soon, and add these to your daily Homework list.

4. Make a note of any other commitments you have today, such as sports, extracurricular activities, or appointments.

5. Based on priorities, time needed, and your own preference, fill out the "Work Plan" timesheet.
    *   Do you want to knock out some quick or easy homework items first before tackling the bigger assignments?
    *   Schedule in breaks where you need them!

6. Finally, most important: Write down three good things about yourself.
    *   This is part of your homework.
    *   Don't be boring. Take a minute and give yourself a good look each day. Challenge yourself to be creative and honest (no holding back on your good stuff!)

Tuesday, Date: 10-9-18

BULLETPROOF

Homework

Class: Chemistry	Due	10-10
Read chapter 4, do problems 1-9	Priority	1
	Time	45

Class: Geometry	Due	10-10
Page 112, odd problems 1-19	Priority	1
	Time	45

Class: English	Due	10-10
Odyssey book 9	Priority	1
Quiz tomorrow	Time	30

Class: Spanish	Due	10-12
	Priority	3
Permission slip	Time	5

Class: History	Due	10-10
Read chapter 6, pages 201-203	Priority	1
Silk Road worksheet	Time	30

Class: Drawing	Due	
	Priority	
None!	Time	

Class:	Due	
	Priority	
	Time	

Heads up! Future due dates and tests:
Chem test Friday

History research paper due December 10 — topic due this Friday

What other commitments do I have today?
Cross country practice

Where do I need help?

Work Plan

3:00	XC practice
3:15	
3:30	
3:45	
4:00	
4:15	
4:30	
4:45	
5:00	
5:15	
5:30	Break
5:45	
6:00	Dinner
6:15	
6:30	English
6:45	
7:00	History
7:15	
7:30	Break
7:45	Geometry
8:00	
8:15	
8:30	Break
8:45	Chemistry
9:00	
9:15	
9:30	*Mom permission slip
9:45	
10:00	
10:15	
10:30	
10:45	

Three good things about me:

I'm funny

I fixed up Jake for the homecoming dance

I can whistle with my fingers

HIGH PERFORMANCE BULLETPROOF TIPS

1. Set Goals
    *   Set goals for yourself, write them down, and share them with someone. Think through your academic and life goals. Do you want to get at least a "B" in all of your classes by the end of the semester, or just not be on academic probation? Do you want to make the basketball team? Make a new friend? Write it down.
    *   Each month, set one or more meaningful goals for yourself on the Monthly Calendar page. These support your big goals. Reminding yourself about your goals and breaking big ones into smaller chunks makes them more achievable. At the end of the month, assess how you did for each of your monthly goals.
    *   Each week, on Sunday, set one or more small goals for the week ahead. Keep these in your sights for the next week.
    *   Stack your goals so that you have short term goals that contribute to your longer term goals. For example, "Do all my chemistry homework" and "Review chemistry class notes for 15 minutes each day" both contribute to a larger goal of "Pass the chemistry exam" or "Get an A in Chemistry".
    *   Good goals are a stretch or a challenge, but keep your goals realistic and achievable.

2. Be proactive with planning long-term projects so they don't sneak up and dump an impossible load of work on you the night before they're due.
    *   Look over the project carefully <u>the day it is assigned</u>, to get a sense of how much work is involved.
    *   Break it down into bite size pieces.
    *   Plan backwards from the due date, setting milestones for specific parts of the project along the way.
    *   Schedule time each day or week to work on the milestone tasks.

3. Successful people ASK FOR HELP when they need it.
    *   Ask a teacher if you don't understand something, are having trouble in the class, or are behind on your homework. Most will meet you more than halfway if you will just ask.
    *   If you are struggling and you feel that you can't talk to the teacher, ask your counselor for advice. They are a professional, trained to coach you in exactly this sort of problem.
    *   Don't let feeling awkward stand in the way of getting what you want. Get over it, and get what you want. Once you have done it a few times it gets so much easier.

4. Energy and time are limited resources. Make sure you take care of your priorities first. Do yourself a favor and save Snapchat and video games, etc. until after your homework is done.

5. Limit distractions. Put your phone away, far away, so that you can get yourself focused and in the zone for homework. You will work so much faster if you are not constantly interrupted. All those little beeps and dings add up.

BULLETPROOF MONTHLY CALENDARS

Month: _____

Monday	Tuesday	Wednesday	Thursday

Plan backwards for big projects!

BULLETPROOF

Friday	Saturday	Sunday	My Goals

Month: _____

Monday	Tuesday	Wednesday	Thursday

Plan backwards for big projects!

BULLETPROOF

Friday	Saturday	Sunday	My Goals

Month: _____

Monday	Tuesday	Wednesday	Thursday

Plan backwards for big projects!

Friday	Saturday	Sunday	My Goals

Month: _____

Monday	Tuesday	Wednesday	Thursday

Plan backwards for big projects!

BULLETPROOF

Friday	Saturday	Sunday	My Goals

Month: _____

Monday	Tuesday	Wednesday	Thursday

Plan backwards for big projects!

BULLETPROOF

Friday	Saturday	Sunday	My Goals

Month: _____

Monday	Tuesday	Wednesday	Thursday

Plan backwards for big projects!

Friday	Saturday	Sunday	My Goals

Bulletproof Daily Homework

Monday, Date: _____

Homework

Class:	Due	
	Priority	
	Time	
Class:	Due	
	Priority	
	Time	
Class:	Due	
	Priority	
	Time	
Class:	Due	
	Priority	
	Time	
Class:	Due	
	Priority	
	Time	
Class:	Due	
	Priority	
	Time	
Class:	Due	
	Priority	
	Time	

Heads up! Future due dates and tests:

What other commitments do I have today?

Where do I need help?

Work Plan

3:00	
3:15	
3:30	
3:45	
4:00	
4:15	
4:30	
4:45	
5:00	
5:15	
5:30	
5:45	
6:00	
6:15	
6:30	
6:45	
7:00	
7:15	
7:30	
7:45	
8:00	
8:15	
8:30	
8:45	
9:00	
9:15	
9:30	
9:45	
10:00	
10:15	
10:30	
10:45	

Three good things about me:

Tuesday, Date: _____

Homework

Class:	Due	
	Priority	
	Time	
Class:	Due	
	Priority	
	Time	
Class:	Due	
	Priority	
	Time	
Class:	Due	
	Priority	
	Time	
Class:	Due	
	Priority	
	Time	
Class:	Due	
	Priority	
	Time	
Class:	Due	
	Priority	
	Time	

Heads up! Future due dates and tests:

What other commitments do I have today?

Where do I need help?

Work Plan

3:00
3:15
3:30
3:45
4:00
4:15
4:30
4:45
5:00
5:15
5:30
5:45
6:00
6:15
6:30
6:45
7:00
7:15
7:30
7:45
8:00
8:15
8:30
8:45
9:00
9:15
9:30
9:45
10:00
10:15
10:30
10:45

Three good things about me:

Wednesday, Date: _____

Homework

Class:	Due	
	Priority	
	Time	
Class:	Due	
	Priority	
	Time	
Class:	Due	
	Priority	
	Time	
Class:	Due	
	Priority	
	Time	
Class:	Due	
	Priority	
	Time	
Class:	Due	
	Priority	
	Time	
Class:	Due	
	Priority	
	Time	

Heads up! Future due dates and tests:

What other commitments do I have today?

Where do I need help?

Work Plan

3:00
3:15
3:30
3:45
4:00
4:15
4:30
4:45
5:00
5:15
5:30
5:45
6:00
6:15
6:30
6:45
7:00
7:15
7:30
7:45
8:00
8:15
8:30
8:45
9:00
9:15
9:30
9:45
10:00
10:15
10:30
10:45

Three good things about me:

Thursday, Date: _____

Homework

Class:		Due	
		Priority	
		Time	
Class:		Due	
		Priority	
		Time	
Class:		Due	
		Priority	
		Time	
Class:		Due	
		Priority	
		Time	
Class:		Due	
		Priority	
		Time	
Class:		Due	
		Priority	
		Time	
Class:		Due	
		Priority	
		Time	

Heads up! Future due dates and tests:

What other commitments do I have today?

Where do I need help?

Work Plan

3:00
3:15
3:30
3:45
4:00
4:15
4:30
4:45
5:00
5:15
5:30
5:45
6:00
6:15
6:30
6:45
7:00
7:15
7:30
7:45
8:00
8:15
8:30
8:45
9:00
9:15
9:30
9:45
10:00
10:15
10:30
10:45

Three good things about me:

Friday, Date: _____

Homework

Class:	Due	
	Priority	
	Time	
Class:	Due	
	Priority	
	Time	
Class:	Due	
	Priority	
	Time	
Class:	Due	
	Priority	
	Time	
Class:	Due	
	Priority	
	Time	
Class:	Due	
	Priority	
	Time	
Class:	Due	
	Priority	
	Time	

Heads up! Future due dates and tests:

What other commitments do I have today?

Where do I need help?

Work Plan

3:00	
3:15	
3:30	
3:45	
4:00	
4:15	
4:30	
4:45	
5:00	
5:15	
5:30	
5:45	
6:00	
6:15	
6:30	
6:45	
7:00	
7:15	
7:30	
7:45	
8:00	
8:15	
8:30	
8:45	
9:00	
9:15	
9:30	
9:45	
10:00	
10:15	
10:30	
10:45	

Three good things about me:

Saturday Plan

Time	
8:00	
8:30	
9:00	
9:30	
10:00	
10:30	
11:00	
11:30	
12:00	
12:30	
1:00	
1:30	
2:00	
2:30	
3:00	
3:30	
4:00	
4:30	
5:00	
5:30	
6:00	
6:30	
7:00	
7:30	
8:00	
8:30	
9:00	
9:30	
10:00	
10:30	

Sunday Plan

Time	
8:00	
8:30	
9:00	
9:30	
10:00	
10:30	
11:00	
11:30	
12:00	
12:30	
1:00	
1:30	
2:00	
2:30	
3:00	
3:30	
4:00	
4:30	
5:00	
5:30	
6:00	
6:30	
7:00	
7:30	
8:00	
8:30	
9:00	
9:30	
10:00	
10:30	

What worked this week? Or didn't?

My goals for next week:

Monday, Date: _____

BULLETPROOF

Homework

Class:	Due	
	Priority	
	Time	
Class:	Due	
	Priority	
	Time	
Class:	Due	
	Priority	
	Time	
Class:	Due	
	Priority	
	Time	
Class:	Due	
	Priority	
	Time	
Class:	Due	
	Priority	
	Time	
Class:	Due	
	Priority	
	Time	

Heads up! Future due dates and tests:

What other commitments do I have today?

Where do I need help?

Work Plan

3:00
3:15
3:30
3:45
4:00
4:15
4:30
4:45
5:00
5:15
5:30
5:45
6:00
6:15
6:30
6:45
7:00
7:15
7:30
7:45
8:00
8:15
8:30
8:45
9:00
9:15
9:30
9:45
10:00
10:15
10:30
10:45

Three good things about me:

Tuesday, Date: _____

Homework

Class:	Due	
	Priority	
	Time	
Class:	Due	
	Priority	
	Time	
Class:	Due	
	Priority	
	Time	
Class:	Due	
	Priority	
	Time	
Class:	Due	
	Priority	
	Time	
Class:	Due	
	Priority	
	Time	
Class:	Due	
	Priority	
	Time	

Heads up! Future due dates and tests:

What other commitments do I have today?

Where do I need help?

Work Plan

3:00	
3:15	
3:30	
3:45	
4:00	
4:15	
4:30	
4:45	
5:00	
5:15	
5:30	
5:45	
6:00	
6:15	
6:30	
6:45	
7:00	
7:15	
7:30	
7:45	
8:00	
8:15	
8:30	
8:45	
9:00	
9:15	
9:30	
9:45	
10:00	
10:15	
10:30	
10:45	

Three good things about me:

Wednesday, Date: _____

Homework

Class:			
	Due	
	Priority	
	Time	
Class:	Due	
	Priority	
	Time	
Class:	Due	
	Priority	
	Time	
Class:	Due	
	Priority	
	Time	
Class:	Due	
	Priority	
	Time	
Class:	Due	
	Priority	
	Time	
Class:	Due	
	Priority	
	Time	

Heads up! Future due dates and tests:

What other commitments do I have today?

Where do I need help?

Work Plan

3:00
3:15
3:30
3:45
4:00
4:15
4:30
4:45
5:00
5:15
5:30
5:45
6:00
6:15
6:30
6:45
7:00
7:15
7:30
7:45
8:00
8:15
8:30
8:45
9:00
9:15
9:30
9:45
10:00
10:15
10:30
10:45

Three good things about me:

Thursday, Date: _____

Homework

Class:	Due	
	Priority	
	Time	
Class:	Due	
	Priority	
	Time	
Class:	Due	
	Priority	
	Time	
Class:	Due	
	Priority	
	Time	
Class:	Due	
	Priority	
	Time	
Class:	Due	
	Priority	
	Time	
Class:	Due	
	Priority	
	Time	

Heads up! Future due dates and tests:

What other commitments do I have today?

Where do I need help?

Work Plan

3:00	
3:15	
3:30	
3:45	
4:00	
4:15	
4:30	
4:45	
5:00	
5:15	
5:30	
5:45	
6:00	
6:15	
6:30	
6:45	
7:00	
7:15	
7:30	
7:45	
8:00	
8:15	
8:30	
8:45	
9:00	
9:15	
9:30	
9:45	
10:00	
10:15	
10:30	
10:45	

Three good things about me:

Friday, Date: _____

Homework

Class:		
	Due	
	Priority	
	Time	
Class:	Due	
	Priority	
	Time	
Class:	Due	
	Priority	
	Time	
Class:	Due	
	Priority	
	Time	
Class:	Due	
	Priority	
	Time	
Class:	Due	
	Priority	
	Time	
Class:	Due	
	Priority	
	Time	

Heads up! Future due dates and tests:

What other commitments do I have today?

Where do I need help?

Work Plan

3:00	
3:15	
3:30	
3:45	
4:00	
4:15	
4:30	
4:45	
5:00	
5:15	
5:30	
5:45	
6:00	
6:15	
6:30	
6:45	
7:00	
7:15	
7:30	
7:45	
8:00	
8:15	
8:30	
8:45	
9:00	
9:15	
9:30	
9:45	
10:00	
10:15	
10:30	
10:45	

Three good things about me:

BULLETPROOF

Saturday Plan	
8:00	
8:30	
9:00	
9:30	
10:00	
10:30	
11:00	
11:30	
12:00	
12:30	
1:00	
1:30	
2:00	
2:30	
3:00	
3:30	
4:00	
4:30	
5:00	
5:30	
6:00	
6:30	
7:00	
7:30	
8:00	
8:30	
9:00	
9:30	
10:00	
10:30	

Sunday Plan	
8:00	
8:30	
9:00	
9:30	
10:00	
10:30	
11:00	
11:30	
12:00	
12:30	
1:00	
1:30	
2:00	
2:30	
3:00	
3:30	
4:00	
4:30	
5:00	
5:30	
6:00	
6:30	
7:00	
7:30	
8:00	
8:30	
9:00	
9:30	
10:00	
10:30	

What worked this week? Or didn't?

My goals for next week:

Monday, Date: _____

BULLETPROOF

Homework

Class:		Due	
		Priority	
		Time	
Class:		Due	
		Priority	
		Time	
Class:		Due	
		Priority	
		Time	
Class:		Due	
		Priority	
		Time	
Class:		Due	
		Priority	
		Time	
Class:		Due	
		Priority	
		Time	
Class:		Due	
		Priority	
		Time	

Heads up! Future due dates and tests:

What other commitments do I have today?

Where do I need help?

Work Plan

3:00
3:15
3:30
3:45
4:00
4:15
4:30
4:45
5:00
5:15
5:30
5:45
6:00
6:15
6:30
6:45
7:00
7:15
7:30
7:45
8:00
8:15
8:30
8:45
9:00
9:15
9:30
9:45
10:00
10:15
10:30
10:45

Three good things about me:

Tuesday, Date: _____

Homework

Class:		
	Due	
	Priority	
	Time	
Class:	Due	
	Priority	
	Time	
Class:	Due	
	Priority	
	Time	
Class:	Due	
	Priority	
	Time	
Class:	Due	
	Priority	
	Time	
Class:	Due	
	Priority	
	Time	
Class:	Due	
	Priority	
	Time	

Heads up! Future due dates and tests:

What other commitments do I have today?

Where do I need help?

Work Plan

3:00
3:15
3:30
3:45
4:00
4:15
4:30
4:45
5:00
5:15
5:30
5:45
6:00
6:15
6:30
6:45
7:00
7:15
7:30
7:45
8:00
8:15
8:30
8:45
9:00
9:15
9:30
9:45
10:00
10:15
10:30
10:45

Three good things about me:

Wednesday, Date: _____

Homework

Class:	Due	
	Priority	
	Time	
Class:	Due	
	Priority	
	Time	
Class:	Due	
	Priority	
	Time	
Class:	Due	
	Priority	
	Time	
Class:	Due	
	Priority	
	Time	
Class:	Due	
	Priority	
	Time	
Class:	Due	
	Priority	
	Time	

Heads up! Future due dates and tests:

What other commitments do I have today?

Where do I need help?

Work Plan

3:00
3:15
3:30
3:45
4:00
4:15
4:30
4:45
5:00
5:15
5:30
5:45
6:00
6:15
6:30
6:45
7:00
7:15
7:30
7:45
8:00
8:15
8:30
8:45
9:00
9:15
9:30
9:45
10:00
10:15
10:30
10:45

Three good things about me:

Thursday, Date: _____

Homework

Class:	Due	
	Priority	
	Time	
Class:	Due	
	Priority	
	Time	
Class:	Due	
	Priority	
	Time	
Class:	Due	
	Priority	
	Time	
Class:	Due	
	Priority	
	Time	
Class:	Due	
	Priority	
	Time	
Class:	Due	
	Priority	
	Time	

Heads up! Future due dates and tests:

What other commitments do I have today?

Where do I need help?

Work Plan

3:00
3:15
3:30
3:45
4:00
4:15
4:30
4:45
5:00
5:15
5:30
5:45
6:00
6:15
6:30
6:45
7:00
7:15
7:30
7:45
8:00
8:15
8:30
8:45
9:00
9:15
9:30
9:45
10:00
10:15
10:30
10:45

Three good things about me:

Friday, Date: _____

Homework

Class:	Due	
	Priority	
	Time	
Class:	Due	
	Priority	
	Time	
Class:	Due	
	Priority	
	Time	
Class:	Due	
	Priority	
	Time	
Class:	Due	
	Priority	
	Time	
Class:	Due	
	Priority	
	Time	
Class:	Due	
	Priority	
	Time	

Heads up! Future due dates and tests:

What other commitments do I have today?

Where do I need help?

Work Plan

3:00
3:15
3:30
3:45
4:00
4:15
4:30
4:45
5:00
5:15
5:30
5:45
6:00
6:15
6:30
6:45
7:00
7:15
7:30
7:45
8:00
8:15
8:30
8:45
9:00
9:15
9:30
9:45
10:00
10:15
10:30
10:45

Three good things about me:

BULLETPROOF

Saturday Plan
8:00
8:30
9:00
9:30
10:00
10:30
11:00
11:30
12:00
12:30
1:00
1:30
2:00
2:30
3:00
3:30
4:00
4:30
5:00
5:30
6:00
6:30
7:00
7:30
8:00
8:30
9:00
9:30
10:00
10:30

Sunday Plan
8:00
8:30
9:00
9:30
10:00
10:30
11:00
11:30
12:00
12:30
1:00
1:30
2:00
2:30
3:00
3:30
4:00
4:30
5:00
5:30
6:00
6:30
7:00
7:30
8:00
8:30
9:00
9:30
10:00
10:30

What worked this week? Or didn't?

My goals for next week:

Monday, Date: _____

Homework

Class:	Due	
	Priority	
	Time	
Class:	Due	
	Priority	
	Time	
Class:	Due	
	Priority	
	Time	
Class:	Due	
	Priority	
	Time	
Class:	Due	
	Priority	
	Time	
Class:	Due	
	Priority	
	Time	
Class:	Due	
	Priority	
	Time	

Heads up! Future due dates and tests:

What other commitments do I have today?

Where do I need help?

Work Plan

3:00
3:15
3:30
3:45
4:00
4:15
4:30
4:45
5:00
5:15
5:30
5:45
6:00
6:15
6:30
6:45
7:00
7:15
7:30
7:45
8:00
8:15
8:30
8:45
9:00
9:15
9:30
9:45
10:00
10:15
10:30
10:45

Three good things about me:

Tuesday, Date: _____

BULLETPROOF

Homework

Class:		
	Due	
	Priority	
	Time	
Class:	Due	
	Priority	
	Time	
Class:	Due	
	Priority	
	Time	
Class:	Due	
	Priority	
	Time	
Class:	Due	
	Priority	
	Time	
Class:	Due	
	Priority	
	Time	
Class:	Due	
	Priority	
	Time	

Heads up! Future due dates and tests:

What other commitments do I have today?

Where do I need help?

Work Plan

3:00
3:15
3:30
3:45
4:00
4:15
4:30
4:45
5:00
5:15
5:30
5:45
6:00
6:15
6:30
6:45
7:00
7:15
7:30
7:45
8:00
8:15
8:30
8:45
9:00
9:15
9:30
9:45
10:00
10:15
10:30
10:45

Three good things about me:

Wednesday, Date: _____

Homework

Class:	Due	
	Priority	
	Time	
Class:	Due	
	Priority	
	Time	
Class:	Due	
	Priority	
	Time	
Class:	Due	
	Priority	
	Time	
Class:	Due	
	Priority	
	Time	
Class:	Due	
	Priority	
	Time	
Class:	Due	
	Priority	
	Time	

Heads up! Future due dates and tests:

What other commitments do I have today?

Where do I need help?

Work Plan

3:00	
3:15	
3:30	
3:45	
4:00	
4:15	
4:30	
4:45	
5:00	
5:15	
5:30	
5:45	
6:00	
6:15	
6:30	
6:45	
7:00	
7:15	
7:30	
7:45	
8:00	
8:15	
8:30	
8:45	
9:00	
9:15	
9:30	
9:45	
10:00	
10:15	
10:30	
10:45	

Three good things about me:

Thursday, Date: _____

Homework

Class:		
	Due	
	Priority	
	Time	
Class:	Due	
	Priority	
	Time	
Class:	Due	
	Priority	
	Time	
Class:	Due	
	Priority	
	Time	
Class:	Due	
	Priority	
	Time	
Class:	Due	
	Priority	
	Time	
Class:	Due	
	Priority	
	Time	

Heads up! Future due dates and tests:

What other commitments do I have today?

Where do I need help?

Work Plan

3:00
3:15
3:30
3:45
4:00
4:15
4:30
4:45
5:00
5:15
5:30
5:45
6:00
6:15
6:30
6:45
7:00
7:15
7:30
7:45
8:00
8:15
8:30
8:45
9:00
9:15
9:30
9:45
10:00
10:15
10:30
10:45

Three good things about me:

Friday, Date: _____

Homework

Class:	Due	
	Priority	
	Time	
Class:	Due	
	Priority	
	Time	
Class:	Due	
	Priority	
	Time	
Class:	Due	
	Priority	
	Time	
Class:	Due	
	Priority	
	Time	
Class:	Due	
	Priority	
	Time	
Class:	Due	
	Priority	
	Time	

Heads up! Future due dates and tests:

What other commitments do I have today?

Where do I need help?

Work Plan

3:00	
3:15	
3:30	
3:45	
4:00	
4:15	
4:30	
4:45	
5:00	
5:15	
5:30	
5:45	
6:00	
6:15	
6:30	
6:45	
7:00	
7:15	
7:30	
7:45	
8:00	
8:15	
8:30	
8:45	
9:00	
9:15	
9:30	
9:45	
10:00	
10:15	
10:30	
10:45	

Three good things about me:

BULLETPROOF

Saturday Plan
8:00
8:30
9:00
9:30
10:00
10:30
11:00
11:30
12:00
12:30
1:00
1:30
2:00
2:30
3:00
3:30
4:00
4:30
5:00
5:30
6:00
6:30
7:00
7:30
8:00
8:30
9:00
9:30
10:00
10:30

Sunday Plan
8:00
8:30
9:00
9:30
10:00
10:30
11:00
11:30
12:00
12:30
1:00
1:30
2:00
2:30
3:00
3:30
4:00
4:30
5:00
5:30
6:00
6:30
7:00
7:30
8:00
8:30
9:00
9:30
10:00
10:30

What worked this week? Or didn't?

My goals for next week:

Monday, Date: _____

Homework

Class:	Due	
	Priority	
	Time	
Class:	Due	
	Priority	
	Time	
Class:	Due	
	Priority	
	Time	
Class:	Due	
	Priority	
	Time	
Class:	Due	
	Priority	
	Time	
Class:	Due	
	Priority	
	Time	
Class:	Due	
	Priority	
	Time	

Heads up! Future due dates and tests:

What other commitments do I have today?

Where do I need help?

Work Plan

3:00	
3:15	
3:30	
3:45	
4:00	
4:15	
4:30	
4:45	
5:00	
5:15	
5:30	
5:45	
6:00	
6:15	
6:30	
6:45	
7:00	
7:15	
7:30	
7:45	
8:00	
8:15	
8:30	
8:45	
9:00	
9:15	
9:30	
9:45	
10:00	
10:15	
10:30	
10:45	

Three good things about me:

Tuesday, Date: _____

Homework

Class:	Due	
	Priority	
	Time	
Class:	Due	
	Priority	
	Time	
Class:	Due	
	Priority	
	Time	
Class:	Due	
	Priority	
	Time	
Class:	Due	
	Priority	
	Time	
Class:	Due	
	Priority	
	Time	
Class:	Due	
	Priority	
	Time	

Heads up! Future due dates and tests:

What other commitments do I have today?

Where do I need help?

Work Plan

3:00
3:15
3:30
3:45
4:00
4:15
4:30
4:45
5:00
5:15
5:30
5:45
6:00
6:15
6:30
6:45
7:00
7:15
7:30
7:45
8:00
8:15
8:30
8:45
9:00
9:15
9:30
9:45
10:00
10:15
10:30
10:45

Three good things about me:

Wednesday, Date: _____

Homework

Class:			
	Due		
	Priority		
	Time		
Class:	Due		
	Priority		
	Time		
Class:	Due		
	Priority		
	Time		
Class:	Due		
	Priority		
	Time		
Class:	Due		
	Priority		
	Time		
Class:	Due		
	Priority		
	Time		
Class:	Due		
	Priority		
	Time		

Heads up! Future due dates and tests:

What other commitments do I have today?

Where do I need help?

Work Plan

3:00	
3:15	
3:30	
3:45	
4:00	
4:15	
4:30	
4:45	
5:00	
5:15	
5:30	
5:45	
6:00	
6:15	
6:30	
6:45	
7:00	
7:15	
7:30	
7:45	
8:00	
8:15	
8:30	
8:45	
9:00	
9:15	
9:30	
9:45	
10:00	
10:15	
10:30	
10:45	

Three good things about me:

Thursday, Date: _____

Homework

Class:	Due	
	Priority	
	Time	
Class:	Due	
	Priority	
	Time	
Class:	Due	
	Priority	
	Time	
Class:	Due	
	Priority	
	Time	
Class:	Due	
	Priority	
	Time	
Class:	Due	
	Priority	
	Time	
Class:	Due	
	Priority	
	Time	

Heads up! Future due dates and tests:

What other commitments do I have today?

Where do I need help?

Work Plan

3:00	
3:15	
3:30	
3:45	
4:00	
4:15	
4:30	
4:45	
5:00	
5:15	
5:30	
5:45	
6:00	
6:15	
6:30	
6:45	
7:00	
7:15	
7:30	
7:45	
8:00	
8:15	
8:30	
8:45	
9:00	
9:15	
9:30	
9:45	
10:00	
10:15	
10:30	
10:45	

Three good things about me:

Friday, Date: _____

BULLETPROOF

Homework

Class:		
	Due	
	Priority	
	Time	
Class:	Due	
	Priority	
	Time	
Class:	Due	
	Priority	
	Time	
Class:	Due	
	Priority	
	Time	
Class:	Due	
	Priority	
	Time	
Class:	Due	
	Priority	
	Time	
Class:	Due	
	Priority	
	Time	

Heads up! Future due dates and tests:

What other commitments do I have today?

Where do I need help?

Work Plan

3:00
3:15
3:30
3:45
4:00
4:15
4:30
4:45
5:00
5:15
5:30
5:45
6:00
6:15
6:30
6:45
7:00
7:15
7:30
7:45
8:00
8:15
8:30
8:45
9:00
9:15
9:30
9:45
10:00
10:15
10:30
10:45

Three good things about me:

BULLETPROOF

Saturday Plan
8:00
8:30
9:00
9:30
10:00
10:30
11:00
11:30
12:00
12:30
1:00
1:30
2:00
2:30
3:00
3:30
4:00
4:30
5:00
5:30
6:00
6:30
7:00
7:30
8:00
8:30
9:00
9:30
10:00
10:30

Sunday Plan
8:00
8:30
9:00
9:30
10:00
10:30
11:00
11:30
12:00
12:30
1:00
1:30
2:00
2:30
3:00
3:30
4:00
4:30
5:00
5:30
6:00
6:30
7:00
7:30
8:00
8:30
9:00
9:30
10:00
10:30

What worked this week? Or didn't?

My goals for next week:

Monday, Date: _____

Homework

Class:	Due	
	Priority	
	Time	
Class:	Due	
	Priority	
	Time	
Class:	Due	
	Priority	
	Time	
Class:	Due	
	Priority	
	Time	
Class:	Due	
	Priority	
	Time	
Class:	Due	
	Priority	
	Time	
Class:	Due	
	Priority	
	Time	

Work Plan

3:00
3:15
3:30
3:45
4:00
4:15
4:30
4:45
5:00
5:15
5:30
5:45
6:00
6:15
6:30
6:45
7:00
7:15
7:30
7:45
8:00
8:15
8:30
8:45
9:00
9:15
9:30
9:45
10:00
10:15
10:30
10:45

Heads up! Future due dates and tests:

What other commitments do I have today?

Where do I need help?

Three good things about me:

Tuesday, Date: _____

Homework

Class:			
	Due	
	Priority	
	Time	
Class:	Due	
	Priority	
	Time	
Class:	Due	
	Priority	
	Time	
Class:	Due	
	Priority	
	Time	
Class:	Due	
	Priority	
	Time	
Class:	Due	
	Priority	
	Time	
Class:	Due	
	Priority	
	Time	

Heads up! Future due dates and tests:

What other commitments do I have today?

Where do I need help?

Work Plan

3:00	
3:15	
3:30	
3:45	
4:00	
4:15	
4:30	
4:45	
5:00	
5:15	
5:30	
5:45	
6:00	
6:15	
6:30	
6:45	
7:00	
7:15	
7:30	
7:45	
8:00	
8:15	
8:30	
8:45	
9:00	
9:15	
9:30	
9:45	
10:00	
10:15	
10:30	
10:45	

Three good things about me:

Wednesday, Date: _____

Homework

Class:			
	Due	
	Priority	
	Time	
Class:	Due	
	Priority	
	Time	
Class:	Due	
	Priority	
	Time	
Class:	Due	
	Priority	
	Time	
Class:	Due	
	Priority	
	Time	
Class:	Due	
	Priority	
	Time	
Class:	Due	
	Priority	
	Time	

Heads up! Future due dates and tests:

What other commitments do I have today?

Where do I need help?

Work Plan

3:00	
3:15	
3:30	
3:45	
4:00	
4:15	
4:30	
4:45	
5:00	
5:15	
5:30	
5:45	
6:00	
6:15	
6:30	
6:45	
7:00	
7:15	
7:30	
7:45	
8:00	
8:15	
8:30	
8:45	
9:00	
9:15	
9:30	
9:45	
10:00	
10:15	
10:30	
10:45	

Three good things about me:

Thursday, Date: _____

Homework

Class:	Due	
	Priority	
	Time	
Class:	Due	
	Priority	
	Time	
Class:	Due	
	Priority	
	Time	
Class:	Due	
	Priority	
	Time	
Class:	Due	
	Priority	
	Time	
Class:	Due	
	Priority	
	Time	
Class:	Due	
	Priority	
	Time	

Heads up! Future due dates and tests:

What other commitments do I have today?

Where do I need help?

Work Plan

3:00
3:15
3:30
3:45
4:00
4:15
4:30
4:45
5:00
5:15
5:30
5:45
6:00
6:15
6:30
6:45
7:00
7:15
7:30
7:45
8:00
8:15
8:30
8:45
9:00
9:15
9:30
9:45
10:00
10:15
10:30
10:45

Three good things about me:

Friday, Date: _____

Homework

Class:	Due	
	Priority	
	Time	
Class:	Due	
	Priority	
	Time	
Class:	Due	
	Priority	
	Time	
Class:	Due	
	Priority	
	Time	
Class:	Due	
	Priority	
	Time	
Class:	Due	
	Priority	
	Time	
Class:	Due	
	Priority	
	Time	

Heads up! Future due dates and tests:

What other commitments do I have today?

Where do I need help?

Work Plan

3:00
3:15
3:30
3:45
4:00
4:15
4:30
4:45
5:00
5:15
5:30
5:45
6:00
6:15
6:30
6:45
7:00
7:15
7:30
7:45
8:00
8:15
8:30
8:45
9:00
9:15
9:30
9:45
10:00
10:15
10:30
10:45

Three good things about me:

BULLETPROOF

Saturday Plan	
8:00	
8:30	
9:00	
9:30	
10:00	
10:30	
11:00	
11:30	
12:00	
12:30	
1:00	
1:30	
2:00	
2:30	
3:00	
3:30	
4:00	
4:30	
5:00	
5:30	
6:00	
6:30	
7:00	
7:30	
8:00	
8:30	
9:00	
9:30	
10:00	
10:30	

Sunday Plan	
8:00	
8:30	
9:00	
9:30	
10:00	
10:30	
11:00	
11:30	
12:00	
12:30	
1:00	
1:30	
2:00	
2:30	
3:00	
3:30	
4:00	
4:30	
5:00	
5:30	
6:00	
6:30	
7:00	
7:30	
8:00	
8:30	
9:00	
9:30	
10:00	
10:30	

What worked this week? Or didn't?

My goals for next week:

Monday, Date: _____

Homework

Class:			
	Due	
	Priority	
	Time	
Class:	Due	
	Priority	
	Time	
Class:	Due	
	Priority	
	Time	
Class:	Due	
	Priority	
	Time	
Class:	Due	
	Priority	
	Time	
Class:	Due	
	Priority	
	Time	
Class:	Due	
	Priority	
	Time	

Heads up! Future due dates and tests:

What other commitments do I have today?

Where do I need help?

Work Plan

3:00	
3:15	
3:30	
3:45	
4:00	
4:15	
4:30	
4:45	
5:00	
5:15	
5:30	
5:45	
6:00	
6:15	
6:30	
6:45	
7:00	
7:15	
7:30	
7:45	
8:00	
8:15	
8:30	
8:45	
9:00	
9:15	
9:30	
9:45	
10:00	
10:15	
10:30	
10:45	

Three good things about me:

Tuesday, Date: _____

Homework

Class:		Due	
		Priority	
		Time	
Class:		Due	
		Priority	
		Time	
Class:		Due	
		Priority	
		Time	
Class:		Due	
		Priority	
		Time	
Class:		Due	
		Priority	
		Time	
Class:		Due	
		Priority	
		Time	
Class:		Due	
		Priority	
		Time	

Heads up! Future due dates and tests:

What other commitments do I have today?

Where do I need help?

Work Plan

3:00
3:15
3:30
3:45
4:00
4:15
4:30
4:45
5:00
5:15
5:30
5:45
6:00
6:15
6:30
6:45
7:00
7:15
7:30
7:45
8:00
8:15
8:30
8:45
9:00
9:15
9:30
9:45
10:00
10:15
10:30
10:45

Three good things about me:

Wednesday, Date: _____

BULLETPROOF

Homework

Class:	Due	
	Priority	
	Time	
Class:	Due	
	Priority	
	Time	
Class:	Due	
	Priority	
	Time	
Class:	Due	
	Priority	
	Time	
Class:	Due	
	Priority	
	Time	
Class:	Due	
	Priority	
	Time	
Class:	Due	
	Priority	
	Time	

Heads up! Future due dates and tests:

What other commitments do I have today?

Where do I need help?

Work Plan

3:00
3:15
3:30
3:45
4:00
4:15
4:30
4:45
5:00
5:15
5:30
5:45
6:00
6:15
6:30
6:45
7:00
7:15
7:30
7:45
8:00
8:15
8:30
8:45
9:00
9:15
9:30
9:45
10:00
10:15
10:30
10:45

Three good things about me:

Thursday, Date: _____

Homework

Class:	Due	
	Priority	
	Time	
Class:	Due	
	Priority	
	Time	
Class:	Due	
	Priority	
	Time	
Class:	Due	
	Priority	
	Time	
Class:	Due	
	Priority	
	Time	
Class:	Due	
	Priority	
	Time	
Class:	Due	
	Priority	
	Time	

Work Plan

3:00
3:15
3:30
3:45
4:00
4:15
4:30
4:45
5:00
5:15
5:30
5:45
6:00
6:15
6:30
6:45
7:00
7:15
7:30
7:45
8:00
8:15
8:30
8:45
9:00
9:15
9:30
9:45
10:00
10:15
10:30
10:45

Heads up! Future due dates and tests:

What other commitments do I have today?

Where do I need help?

Three good things about me:

Friday, Date: _____

Homework

Class:	Due	
	Priority	
	Time	
Class:	Due	
	Priority	
	Time	
Class:	Due	
	Priority	
	Time	
Class:	Due	
	Priority	
	Time	
Class:	Due	
	Priority	
	Time	
Class:	Due	
	Priority	
	Time	
Class:	Due	
	Priority	
	Time	

Heads up! Future due dates and tests:

What other commitments do I have today?

Where do I need help?

Work Plan

3:00	
3:15	
3:30	
3:45	
4:00	
4:15	
4:30	
4:45	
5:00	
5:15	
5:30	
5:45	
6:00	
6:15	
6:30	
6:45	
7:00	
7:15	
7:30	
7:45	
8:00	
8:15	
8:30	
8:45	
9:00	
9:15	
9:30	
9:45	
10:00	
10:15	
10:30	
10:45	

Three good things about me:

Saturday Plan	
8:00	
8:30	
9:00	
9:30	
10:00	
10:30	
11:00	
11:30	
12:00	
12:30	
1:00	
1:30	
2:00	
2:30	
3:00	
3:30	
4:00	
4:30	
5:00	
5:30	
6:00	
6:30	
7:00	
7:30	
8:00	
8:30	
9:00	
9:30	
10:00	
10:30	

Sunday Plan	
8:00	
8:30	
9:00	
9:30	
10:00	
10:30	
11:00	
11:30	
12:00	
12:30	
1:00	
1:30	
2:00	
2:30	
3:00	
3:30	
4:00	
4:30	
5:00	
5:30	
6:00	
6:30	
7:00	
7:30	
8:00	
8:30	
9:00	
9:30	
10:00	
10:30	

What worked this week? Or didn't?

My goals for next week:

Monday, Date: _____

Homework

Class:	Due	
	Priority	
	Time	
Class:	Due	
	Priority	
	Time	
Class:	Due	
	Priority	
	Time	
Class:	Due	
	Priority	
	Time	
Class:	Due	
	Priority	
	Time	
Class:	Due	
	Priority	
	Time	
Class:	Due	
	Priority	
	Time	

Heads up! Future due dates and tests:

What other commitments do I have today?

Where do I need help?

Work Plan

3:00
3:15
3:30
3:45
4:00
4:15
4:30
4:45
5:00
5:15
5:30
5:45
6:00
6:15
6:30
6:45
7:00
7:15
7:30
7:45
8:00
8:15
8:30
8:45
9:00
9:15
9:30
9:45
10:00
10:15
10:30
10:45

Three good things about me:

Tuesday, Date: _____

BULLETPROOF

Homework

Class:		
	Due	
	Priority	
	Time	
Class:	Due	
	Priority	
	Time	
Class:	Due	
	Priority	
	Time	
Class:	Due	
	Priority	
	Time	
Class:	Due	
	Priority	
	Time	
Class:	Due	
	Priority	
	Time	
Class:	Due	
	Priority	
	Time	

Heads up! Future due dates and tests:

What other commitments do I have today?

Where do I need help?

Work Plan

3:00
3:15
3:30
3:45
4:00
4:15
4:30
4:45
5:00
5:15
5:30
5:45
6:00
6:15
6:30
6:45
7:00
7:15
7:30
7:45
8:00
8:15
8:30
8:45
9:00
9:15
9:30
9:45
10:00
10:15
10:30
10:45

Three good things about me:

Wednesday, Date: _____

Homework

Class:	Due	
	Priority	
	Time	
Class:	Due	
	Priority	
	Time	
Class:	Due	
	Priority	
	Time	
Class:	Due	
	Priority	
	Time	
Class:	Due	
	Priority	
	Time	
Class:	Due	
	Priority	
	Time	
Class:	Due	
	Priority	
	Time	

Heads up! Future due dates and tests:

What other commitments do I have today?

Where do I need help?

Work Plan

| **3:00** |
| 3:15 |
| 3:30 |
| 3:45 |
| **4:00** |
| 4:15 |
| 4:30 |
| 4:45 |
| **5:00** |
| 5:15 |
| 5:30 |
| 5:45 |
| **6:00** |
| 6:15 |
| 6:30 |
| 6:45 |
| **7:00** |
| 7:15 |
| 7:30 |
| 7:45 |
| **8:00** |
| 8:15 |
| 8:30 |
| 8:45 |
| **9:00** |
| 9:15 |
| 9:30 |
| 9:45 |
| **10:00** |
| 10:15 |
| 10:30 |
| 10:45 |

Three good things about me:

Thursday, Date: _____

Homework

Class:		Due	
		Priority	
		Time	
Class:		Due	
		Priority	
		Time	
Class:		Due	
		Priority	
		Time	
Class:		Due	
		Priority	
		Time	
Class:		Due	
		Priority	
		Time	
Class:		Due	
		Priority	
		Time	
Class:		Due	
		Priority	
		Time	

Heads up! Future due dates and tests:

What other commitments do I have today?

Where do I need help?

Work Plan

3:00
3:15
3:30
3:45
4:00
4:15
4:30
4:45
5:00
5:15
5:30
5:45
6:00
6:15
6:30
6:45
7:00
7:15
7:30
7:45
8:00
8:15
8:30
8:45
9:00
9:15
9:30
9:45
10:00
10:15
10:30
10:45

Three good things about me:

Friday, Date: _____

Homework

Class:	Due	
	Priority	
	Time	
Class:	Due	
	Priority	
	Time	
Class:	Due	
	Priority	
	Time	
Class:	Due	
	Priority	
	Time	
Class:	Due	
	Priority	
	Time	
Class:	Due	
	Priority	
	Time	
Class:	Due	
	Priority	
	Time	

Heads up! Future due dates and tests:

What other commitments do I have today?

Where do I need help?

Work Plan

| **3:00** |
| 3:15 |
| 3:30 |
| 3:45 |
| **4:00** |
| 4:15 |
| 4:30 |
| 4:45 |
| **5:00** |
| 5:15 |
| 5:30 |
| 5:45 |
| **6:00** |
| 6:15 |
| 6:30 |
| 6:45 |
| **7:00** |
| 7:15 |
| 7:30 |
| 7:45 |
| **8:00** |
| 8:15 |
| 8:30 |
| 8:45 |
| **9:00** |
| 9:15 |
| 9:30 |
| 9:45 |
| **10:00** |
| 10:15 |
| 10:30 |
| 10:45 |

Three good things about me:

BULLETPROOF

Saturday Plan
8:00
8:30
9:00
9:30
10:00
10:30
11:00
11:30
12:00
12:30
1:00
1:30
2:00
2:30
3:00
3:30
4:00
4:30
5:00
5:30
6:00
6:30
7:00
7:30
8:00
8:30
9:00
9:30
10:00
10:30

Sunday Plan
8:00
8:30
9:00
9:30
10:00
10:30
11:00
11:30
12:00
12:30
1:00
1:30
2:00
2:30
3:00
3:30
4:00
4:30
5:00
5:30
6:00
6:30
7:00
7:30
8:00
8:30
9:00
9:30
10:00
10:30

What worked this week? Or didn't?

My goals for next week:

Monday, Date: _____

Homework

Class:	Due	
	Priority	
	Time	
Class:	Due	
	Priority	
	Time	
Class:	Due	
	Priority	
	Time	
Class:	Due	
	Priority	
	Time	
Class:	Due	
	Priority	
	Time	
Class:	Due	
	Priority	
	Time	
Class:	Due	
	Priority	
	Time	

Heads up! Future due dates and tests:

What other commitments do I have today?

Where do I need help?

Work Plan

3:00
3:15
3:30
3:45
4:00
4:15
4:30
4:45
5:00
5:15
5:30
5:45
6:00
6:15
6:30
6:45
7:00
7:15
7:30
7:45
8:00
8:15
8:30
8:45
9:00
9:15
9:30
9:45
10:00
10:15
10:30
10:45

Three good things about me:

Tuesday, Date: _____

Homework

Class:			
	Due	
	Priority	
	Time	
Class:	Due	
	Priority	
	Time	
Class:	Due	
	Priority	
	Time	
Class:	Due	
	Priority	
	Time	
Class:	Due	
	Priority	
	Time	
Class:	Due	
	Priority	
	Time	
Class:	Due	
	Priority	
	Time	

Heads up! Future due dates and tests:

What other commitments do I have today?

Where do I need help?

Work Plan

3:00
3:15
3:30
3:45
4:00
4:15
4:30
4:45
5:00
5:15
5:30
5:45
6:00
6:15
6:30
6:45
7:00
7:15
7:30
7:45
8:00
8:15
8:30
8:45
9:00
9:15
9:30
9:45
10:00
10:15
10:30
10:45

Three good things about me:

Wednesday, Date: _____

Homework

Class:	Due	
	Priority	
	Time	
Class:	Due	
	Priority	
	Time	
Class:	Due	
	Priority	
	Time	
Class:	Due	
	Priority	
	Time	
Class:	Due	
	Priority	
	Time	
Class:	Due	
	Priority	
	Time	
Class:	Due	
	Priority	
	Time	

Heads up! Future due dates and tests:

What other commitments do I have today?

Where do I need help?

Work Plan

3:00
3:15
3:30
3:45
4:00
4:15
4:30
4:45
5:00
5:15
5:30
5:45
6:00
6:15
6:30
6:45
7:00
7:15
7:30
7:45
8:00
8:15
8:30
8:45
9:00
9:15
9:30
9:45
10:00
10:15
10:30
10:45

Three good things about me:

Thursday, Date: _____

Homework

Class:	Due	
	Priority	
	Time	
Class:	Due	
	Priority	
	Time	
Class:	Due	
	Priority	
	Time	
Class:	Due	
	Priority	
	Time	
Class:	Due	
	Priority	
	Time	
Class:	Due	
	Priority	
	Time	
Class:	Due	
	Priority	
	Time	

Heads up! Future due dates and tests:

What other commitments do I have today?

Where do I need help?

Work Plan

3:00	
3:15	
3:30	
3:45	
4:00	
4:15	
4:30	
4:45	
5:00	
5:15	
5:30	
5:45	
6:00	
6:15	
6:30	
6:45	
7:00	
7:15	
7:30	
7:45	
8:00	
8:15	
8:30	
8:45	
9:00	
9:15	
9:30	
9:45	
10:00	
10:15	
10:30	
10:45	

Three good things about me:

Friday, Date: _____

Homework

Class:	Due	
	Priority	
	Time	
Class:	Due	
	Priority	
	Time	
Class:	Due	
	Priority	
	Time	
Class:	Due	
	Priority	
	Time	
Class:	Due	
	Priority	
	Time	
Class:	Due	
	Priority	
	Time	
Class:	Due	
	Priority	
	Time	

Heads up! Future due dates and tests:

What other commitments do I have today?

Where do I need help?

Work Plan

3:00
3:15
3:30
3:45
4:00
4:15
4:30
4:45
5:00
5:15
5:30
5:45
6:00
6:15
6:30
6:45
7:00
7:15
7:30
7:45
8:00
8:15
8:30
8:45
9:00
9:15
9:30
9:45
10:00
10:15
10:30
10:45

Three good things about me:

BULLETPROOF

Saturday Plan
8:00
8:30
9:00
9:30
10:00
10:30
11:00
11:30
12:00
12:30
1:00
1:30
2:00
2:30
3:00
3:30
4:00
4:30
5:00
5:30
6:00
6:30
7:00
7:30
8:00
8:30
9:00
9:30
10:00
10:30

Sunday Plan
8:00
8:30
9:00
9:30
10:00
10:30
11:00
11:30
12:00
12:30
1:00
1:30
2:00
2:30
3:00
3:30
4:00
4:30
5:00
5:30
6:00
6:30
7:00
7:30
8:00
8:30
9:00
9:30
10:00
10:30

What worked this week? Or didn't?

My goals for next week:

Monday, Date: _____

Homework

Class:	Due	
	Priority	
	Time	
Class:	Due	
	Priority	
	Time	
Class:	Due	
	Priority	
	Time	
Class:	Due	
	Priority	
	Time	
Class:	Due	
	Priority	
	Time	
Class:	Due	
	Priority	
	Time	
Class:	Due	
	Priority	
	Time	

Heads up! Future due dates and tests:

What other commitments do I have today?

Where do I need help?

Work Plan

3:00	
3:15	
3:30	
3:45	
4:00	
4:15	
4:30	
4:45	
5:00	
5:15	
5:30	
5:45	
6:00	
6:15	
6:30	
6:45	
7:00	
7:15	
7:30	
7:45	
8:00	
8:15	
8:30	
8:45	
9:00	
9:15	
9:30	
9:45	
10:00	
10:15	
10:30	
10:45	

Three good things about me:

Tuesday, Date: _____

Homework

Class:	Due	
	Priority	
	Time	
Class:	Due	
	Priority	
	Time	
Class:	Due	
	Priority	
	Time	
Class:	Due	
	Priority	
	Time	
Class:	Due	
	Priority	
	Time	
Class:	Due	
	Priority	
	Time	
Class:	Due	
	Priority	
	Time	

Heads up! Future due dates and tests:

What other commitments do I have today?

Where do I need help?

Work Plan

3:00	
3:15	
3:30	
3:45	
4:00	
4:15	
4:30	
4:45	
5:00	
5:15	
5:30	
5:45	
6:00	
6:15	
6:30	
6:45	
7:00	
7:15	
7:30	
7:45	
8:00	
8:15	
8:30	
8:45	
9:00	
9:15	
9:30	
9:45	
10:00	
10:15	
10:30	
10:45	

Three good things about me:

Wednesday, Date: _____

BULLETPROOF

Homework

Class:	Due	
	Priority	
	Time	
Class:	Due	
	Priority	
	Time	
Class:	Due	
	Priority	
	Time	
Class:	Due	
	Priority	
	Time	
Class:	Due	
	Priority	
	Time	
Class:	Due	
	Priority	
	Time	
Class:	Due	
	Priority	
	Time	

Heads up! Future due dates and tests:

What other commitments do I have today?

Where do I need help?

Work Plan

3:00
3:15
3:30
3:45
4:00
4:15
4:30
4:45
5:00
5:15
5:30
5:45
6:00
6:15
6:30
6:45
7:00
7:15
7:30
7:45
8:00
8:15
8:30
8:45
9:00
9:15
9:30
9:45
10:00
10:15
10:30
10:45

Three good things about me:

Thursday, Date: _____

Homework

Class:	Due	
	Priority	
	Time	
Class:	Due	
	Priority	
	Time	
Class:	Due	
	Priority	
	Time	
Class:	Due	
	Priority	
	Time	
Class:	Due	
	Priority	
	Time	
Class:	Due	
	Priority	
	Time	
Class:	Due	
	Priority	
	Time	

Heads up! Future due dates and tests:

What other commitments do I have today?

Where do I need help?

Work Plan

3:00
3:15
3:30
3:45
4:00
4:15
4:30
4:45
5:00
5:15
5:30
5:45
6:00
6:15
6:30
6:45
7:00
7:15
7:30
7:45
8:00
8:15
8:30
8:45
9:00
9:15
9:30
9:45
10:00
10:15
10:30
10:45

Three good things about me:

Friday, Date: _____

Homework

Class:	Due	
	Priority	
	Time	
Class:	Due	
	Priority	
	Time	
Class:	Due	
	Priority	
	Time	
Class:	Due	
	Priority	
	Time	
Class:	Due	
	Priority	
	Time	
Class:	Due	
	Priority	
	Time	
Class:	Due	
	Priority	
	Time	

Heads up! Future due dates and tests:

What other commitments do I have today?

Where do I need help?

Work Plan

3:00
3:15
3:30
3:45
4:00
4:15
4:30
4:45
5:00
5:15
5:30
5:45
6:00
6:15
6:30
6:45
7:00
7:15
7:30
7:45
8:00
8:15
8:30
8:45
9:00
9:15
9:30
9:45
10:00
10:15
10:30
10:45

Three good things about me:

BULLETPROOF

Saturday Plan	
8:00	
8:30	
9:00	
9:30	
10:00	
10:30	
11:00	
11:30	
12:00	
12:30	
1:00	
1:30	
2:00	
2:30	
3:00	
3:30	
4:00	
4:30	
5:00	
5:30	
6:00	
6:30	
7:00	
7:30	
8:00	
8:30	
9:00	
9:30	
10:00	
10:30	

Sunday Plan	
8:00	
8:30	
9:00	
9:30	
10:00	
10:30	
11:00	
11:30	
12:00	
12:30	
1:00	
1:30	
2:00	
2:30	
3:00	
3:30	
4:00	
4:30	
5:00	
5:30	
6:00	
6:30	
7:00	
7:30	
8:00	
8:30	
9:00	
9:30	
10:00	
10:30	

What worked this week? Or didn't?

My goals for next week:

Monday, Date: _____

Homework

Class:	Due	
	Priority	
	Time	
Class:	Due	
	Priority	
	Time	
Class:	Due	
	Priority	
	Time	
Class:	Due	
	Priority	
	Time	
Class:	Due	
	Priority	
	Time	
Class:	Due	
	Priority	
	Time	
Class:	Due	
	Priority	
	Time	

Heads up! Future due dates and tests:

What other commitments do I have today?

Where do I need help?

Work Plan

3:00	
3:15	
3:30	
3:45	
4:00	
4:15	
4:30	
4:45	
5:00	
5:15	
5:30	
5:45	
6:00	
6:15	
6:30	
6:45	
7:00	
7:15	
7:30	
7:45	
8:00	
8:15	
8:30	
8:45	
9:00	
9:15	
9:30	
9:45	
10:00	
10:15	
10:30	
10:45	

Three good things about me:

Tuesday, Date: _____

Homework

Class:	Due	
	Priority	
	Time	
Class:	Due	
	Priority	
	Time	
Class:	Due	
	Priority	
	Time	
Class:	Due	
	Priority	
	Time	
Class:	Due	
	Priority	
	Time	
Class:	Due	
	Priority	
	Time	
Class:	Due	
	Priority	
	Time	

Heads up! Future due dates and tests:

What other commitments do I have today?

Where do I need help?

Work Plan

3:00
3:15
3:30
3:45
4:00
4:15
4:30
4:45
5:00
5:15
5:30
5:45
6:00
6:15
6:30
6:45
7:00
7:15
7:30
7:45
8:00
8:15
8:30
8:45
9:00
9:15
9:30
9:45
10:00
10:15
10:30
10:45

Three good things about me:

Wednesday, Date: _____

Homework

Class:	Due	
	Priority	
	Time	
Class:	Due	
	Priority	
	Time	
Class:	Due	
	Priority	
	Time	
Class:	Due	
	Priority	
	Time	
Class:	Due	
	Priority	
	Time	
Class:	Due	
	Priority	
	Time	
Class:	Due	
	Priority	
	Time	

Heads up! Future due dates and tests:

What other commitments do I have today?

Where do I need help?

Work Plan

3:00
3:15
3:30
3:45
4:00
4:15
4:30
4:45
5:00
5:15
5:30
5:45
6:00
6:15
6:30
6:45
7:00
7:15
7:30
7:45
8:00
8:15
8:30
8:45
9:00
9:15
9:30
9:45
10:00
10:15
10:30
10:45

Three good things about me:

Thursday, Date: _____

Homework

Class:		Due	
		Priority	
		Time	
Class:		Due	
		Priority	
		Time	
Class:		Due	
		Priority	
		Time	
Class:		Due	
		Priority	
		Time	
Class:		Due	
		Priority	
		Time	
Class:		Due	
		Priority	
		Time	
Class:		Due	
		Priority	
		Time	

Heads up! Future due dates and tests:

What other commitments do I have today?

Where do I need help?

Work Plan

3:00
3:15
3:30
3:45
4:00
4:15
4:30
4:45
5:00
5:15
5:30
5:45
6:00
6:15
6:30
6:45
7:00
7:15
7:30
7:45
8:00
8:15
8:30
8:45
9:00
9:15
9:30
9:45
10:00
10:15
10:30
10:45

Three good things about me:

Friday, Date: _____

BULLETPROOF

Homework

Class:		Due	
		Priority	
		Time	
Class:		Due	
		Priority	
		Time	
Class:		Due	
		Priority	
		Time	
Class:		Due	
		Priority	
		Time	
Class:		Due	
		Priority	
		Time	
Class:		Due	
		Priority	
		Time	
Class:		Due	
		Priority	
		Time	

Heads up! Future due dates and tests:

What other commitments do I have today?

Where do I need help?

Work Plan

3:00
3:15
3:30
3:45
4:00
4:15
4:30
4:45
5:00
5:15
5:30
5:45
6:00
6:15
6:30
6:45
7:00
7:15
7:30
7:45
8:00
8:15
8:30
8:45
9:00
9:15
9:30
9:45
10:00
10:15
10:30
10:45

Three good things about me:

Saturday Plan
8:00
8:30
9:00
9:30
10:00
10:30
11:00
11:30
12:00
12:30
1:00
1:30
2:00
2:30
3:00
3:30
4:00
4:30
5:00
5:30
6:00
6:30
7:00
7:30
8:00
8:30
9:00
9:30
10:00
10:30

Sunday Plan
8:00
8:30
9:00
9:30
10:00
10:30
11:00
11:30
12:00
12:30
1:00
1:30
2:00
2:30
3:00
3:30
4:00
4:30
5:00
5:30
6:00
6:30
7:00
7:30
8:00
8:30
9:00
9:30
10:00
10:30

What worked this week? Or didn't?

My goals for next week:

Monday, Date: _____

Homework

Class:	Due	
	Priority	
	Time	
Class:	Due	
	Priority	
	Time	
Class:	Due	
	Priority	
	Time	
Class:	Due	
	Priority	
	Time	
Class:	Due	
	Priority	
	Time	
Class:	Due	
	Priority	
	Time	
Class:	Due	
	Priority	
	Time	

Heads up! Future due dates and tests:

What other commitments do I have today?

Where do I need help?

Work Plan

3:00
3:15
3:30
3:45
4:00
4:15
4:30
4:45
5:00
5:15
5:30
5:45
6:00
6:15
6:30
6:45
7:00
7:15
7:30
7:45
8:00
8:15
8:30
8:45
9:00
9:15
9:30
9:45
10:00
10:15
10:30
10:45

Three good things about me:

Tuesday, Date: _____

Homework

Class:	Due	
	Priority	
	Time	
Class:	Due	
	Priority	
	Time	
Class:	Due	
	Priority	
	Time	
Class:	Due	
	Priority	
	Time	
Class:	Due	
	Priority	
	Time	
Class:	Due	
	Priority	
	Time	
Class:	Due	
	Priority	
	Time	

Heads up! Future due dates and tests:

What other commitments do I have today?

Where do I need help?

Work Plan

3:00
3:15
3:30
3:45
4:00
4:15
4:30
4:45
5:00
5:15
5:30
5:45
6:00
6:15
6:30
6:45
7:00
7:15
7:30
7:45
8:00
8:15
8:30
8:45
9:00
9:15
9:30
9:45
10:00
10:15
10:30
10:45

Three good things about me:

Wednesday, Date: _____

BULLETPROOF

Homework

Class:	Due	
	Priority	
	Time	
Class:	Due	
	Priority	
	Time	
Class:	Due	
	Priority	
	Time	
Class:	Due	
	Priority	
	Time	
Class:	Due	
	Priority	
	Time	
Class:	Due	
	Priority	
	Time	
Class:	Due	
	Priority	
	Time	

Heads up! Future due dates and tests:

What other commitments do I have today?

Where do I need help?

Work Plan

3:00
3:15
3:30
3:45
4:00
4:15
4:30
4:45
5:00
5:15
5:30
5:45
6:00
6:15
6:30
6:45
7:00
7:15
7:30
7:45
8:00
8:15
8:30
8:45
9:00
9:15
9:30
9:45
10:00
10:15
10:30
10:45

Three good things about me:

Thursday, Date: _____

Homework

Class:			
	Due	
	Priority	
	Time	
Class:	Due	
	Priority	
	Time	
Class:	Due	
	Priority	
	Time	
Class:	Due	
	Priority	
	Time	
Class:	Due	
	Priority	
	Time	
Class:	Due	
	Priority	
	Time	
Class:	Due	
	Priority	
	Time	

Heads up! Future due dates and tests:

What other commitments do I have today?

Where do I need help?

Work Plan

3:00
3:15
3:30
3:45
4:00
4:15
4:30
4:45
5:00
5:15
5:30
5:45
6:00
6:15
6:30
6:45
7:00
7:15
7:30
7:45
8:00
8:15
8:30
8:45
9:00
9:15
9:30
9:45
10:00
10:15
10:30
10:45

Three good things about me:

Friday, Date: _____

Homework

Class:	Due	
	Priority	
	Time	
Class:	Due	
	Priority	
	Time	
Class:	Due	
	Priority	
	Time	
Class:	Due	
	Priority	
	Time	
Class:	Due	
	Priority	
	Time	
Class:	Due	
	Priority	
	Time	
Class:	Due	
	Priority	
	Time	

Heads up! Future due dates and tests:

What other commitments do I have today?

Where do I need help?

Work Plan

3:00
3:15
3:30
3:45
4:00
4:15
4:30
4:45
5:00
5:15
5:30
5:45
6:00
6:15
6:30
6:45
7:00
7:15
7:30
7:45
8:00
8:15
8:30
8:45
9:00
9:15
9:30
9:45
10:00
10:15
10:30
10:45

Three good things about me:

BULLETPROOF

Saturday Plan
8:00
8:30
9:00
9:30
10:00
10:30
11:00
11:30
12:00
12:30
1:00
1:30
2:00
2:30
3:00
3:30
4:00
4:30
5:00
5:30
6:00
6:30
7:00
7:30
8:00
8:30
9:00
9:30
10:00
10:30

Sunday Plan
8:00
8:30
9:00
9:30
10:00
10:30
11:00
11:30
12:00
12:30
1:00
1:30
2:00
2:30
3:00
3:30
4:00
4:30
5:00
5:30
6:00
6:30
7:00
7:30
8:00
8:30
9:00
9:30
10:00
10:30

What worked this week? Or didn't?

My goals for next week:

Monday, Date: _____

BULLETPROOF

Homework

Class:		
	Due	
	Priority	
	Time	
Class:	Due	
	Priority	
	Time	
Class:	Due	
	Priority	
	Time	
Class:	Due	
	Priority	
	Time	
Class:	Due	
	Priority	
	Time	
Class:	Due	
	Priority	
	Time	
Class:	Due	
	Priority	
	Time	

Heads up! Future due dates and tests:

What other commitments do I have today?

Where do I need help?

Work Plan

3:00
3:15
3:30
3:45
4:00
4:15
4:30
4:45
5:00
5:15
5:30
5:45
6:00
6:15
6:30
6:45
7:00
7:15
7:30
7:45
8:00
8:15
8:30
8:45
9:00
9:15
9:30
9:45
10:00
10:15
10:30
10:45

Three good things about me:

Tuesday, Date: _____

Homework

Class:	Due	
	Priority	
	Time	
Class:	Due	
	Priority	
	Time	
Class:	Due	
	Priority	
	Time	
Class:	Due	
	Priority	
	Time	
Class:	Due	
	Priority	
	Time	
Class:	Due	
	Priority	
	Time	
Class:	Due	
	Priority	
	Time	

Heads up! Future due dates and tests:

What other commitments do I have today?

Where do I need help?

Work Plan

3:00
3:15
3:30
3:45
4:00
4:15
4:30
4:45
5:00
5:15
5:30
5:45
6:00
6:15
6:30
6:45
7:00
7:15
7:30
7:45
8:00
8:15
8:30
8:45
9:00
9:15
9:30
9:45
10:00
10:15
10:30
10:45

Three good things about me:

Wednesday, Date: _____

Homework

Class:	Due	
	Priority	
	Time	
Class:	Due	
	Priority	
	Time	
Class:	Due	
	Priority	
	Time	
Class:	Due	
	Priority	
	Time	
Class:	Due	
	Priority	
	Time	
Class:	Due	
	Priority	
	Time	
Class:	Due	
	Priority	
	Time	

Heads up! Future due dates and tests:

What other commitments do I have today?

Where do I need help?

Work Plan

3:00
3:15
3:30
3:45
4:00
4:15
4:30
4:45
5:00
5:15
5:30
5:45
6:00
6:15
6:30
6:45
7:00
7:15
7:30
7:45
8:00
8:15
8:30
8:45
9:00
9:15
9:30
9:45
10:00
10:15
10:30
10:45

Three good things about me:

Thursday, Date: _____

Homework

Class:	Due	
	Priority	
	Time	
Class:	Due	
	Priority	
	Time	
Class:	Due	
	Priority	
	Time	
Class:	Due	
	Priority	
	Time	
Class:	Due	
	Priority	
	Time	
Class:	Due	
	Priority	
	Time	
Class:	Due	
	Priority	
	Time	

Heads up! Future due dates and tests:

What other commitments do I have today?

Where do I need help?

Work Plan

3:00
3:15
3:30
3:45
4:00
4:15
4:30
4:45
5:00
5:15
5:30
5:45
6:00
6:15
6:30
6:45
7:00
7:15
7:30
7:45
8:00
8:15
8:30
8:45
9:00
9:15
9:30
9:45
10:00
10:15
10:30
10:45

Three good things about me:

Friday, Date: _____

Homework

Class:	Due	
	Priority	
	Time	
Class:	Due	
	Priority	
	Time	
Class:	Due	
	Priority	
	Time	
Class:	Due	
	Priority	
	Time	
Class:	Due	
	Priority	
	Time	
Class:	Due	
	Priority	
	Time	
Class:	Due	
	Priority	
	Time	

Heads up! Future due dates and tests:

What other commitments do I have today?

Where do I need help?

Work Plan

3:00	
3:15	
3:30	
3:45	
4:00	
4:15	
4:30	
4:45	
5:00	
5:15	
5:30	
5:45	
6:00	
6:15	
6:30	
6:45	
7:00	
7:15	
7:30	
7:45	
8:00	
8:15	
8:30	
8:45	
9:00	
9:15	
9:30	
9:45	
10:00	
10:15	
10:30	
10:45	

Three good things about me:

Saturday Plan

Time	
8:00	
8:30	
9:00	
9:30	
10:00	
10:30	
11:00	
11:30	
12:00	
12:30	
1:00	
1:30	
2:00	
2:30	
3:00	
3:30	
4:00	
4:30	
5:00	
5:30	
6:00	
6:30	
7:00	
7:30	
8:00	
8:30	
9:00	
9:30	
10:00	
10:30	

Sunday Plan

Time	
8:00	
8:30	
9:00	
9:30	
10:00	
10:30	
11:00	
11:30	
12:00	
12:30	
1:00	
1:30	
2:00	
2:30	
3:00	
3:30	
4:00	
4:30	
5:00	
5:30	
6:00	
6:30	
7:00	
7:30	
8:00	
8:30	
9:00	
9:30	
10:00	
10:30	

What worked this week? Or didn't?

My goals for next week:

Monday, Date: _____

Homework

Class:	Due	
	Priority	
	Time	
Class:	Due	
	Priority	
	Time	
Class:	Due	
	Priority	
	Time	
Class:	Due	
	Priority	
	Time	
Class:	Due	
	Priority	
	Time	
Class:	Due	
	Priority	
	Time	
Class:	Due	
	Priority	
	Time	

Heads up! Future due dates and tests:

What other commitments do I have today?

Where do I need help?

Work Plan

3:00	
3:15	
3:30	
3:45	
4:00	
4:15	
4:30	
4:45	
5:00	
5:15	
5:30	
5:45	
6:00	
6:15	
6:30	
6:45	
7:00	
7:15	
7:30	
7:45	
8:00	
8:15	
8:30	
8:45	
9:00	
9:15	
9:30	
9:45	
10:00	
10:15	
10:30	
10:45	

Three good things about me:

Tuesday, Date: _____

Homework

Class:	Due	
	Priority	
	Time	
Class:	Due	
	Priority	
	Time	
Class:	Due	
	Priority	
	Time	
Class:	Due	
	Priority	
	Time	
Class:	Due	
	Priority	
	Time	
Class:	Due	
	Priority	
	Time	
Class:	Due	
	Priority	
	Time	

Heads up! Future due dates and tests:

What other commitments do I have today?

Where do I need help?

Work Plan

3:00
3:15
3:30
3:45
4:00
4:15
4:30
4:45
5:00
5:15
5:30
5:45
6:00
6:15
6:30
6:45
7:00
7:15
7:30
7:45
8:00
8:15
8:30
8:45
9:00
9:15
9:30
9:45
10:00
10:15
10:30
10:45

Three good things about me:

Wednesday, Date: _____

BULLETPROOF

Homework

Class:	Due	
	Priority	
	Time	
Class:	Due	
	Priority	
	Time	
Class:	Due	
	Priority	
	Time	
Class:	Due	
	Priority	
	Time	
Class:	Due	
	Priority	
	Time	
Class:	Due	
	Priority	
	Time	
Class:	Due	
	Priority	
	Time	

Heads up! Future due dates and tests:

What other commitments do I have today?

Where do I need help?

Work Plan

3:00	
3:15	
3:30	
3:45	
4:00	
4:15	
4:30	
4:45	
5:00	
5:15	
5:30	
5:45	
6:00	
6:15	
6:30	
6:45	
7:00	
7:15	
7:30	
7:45	
8:00	
8:15	
8:30	
8:45	
9:00	
9:15	
9:30	
9:45	
10:00	
10:15	
10:30	
10:45	

Three good things about me:

Thursday, Date: _____

Homework

Class:	Due	
	Priority	
	Time	
Class:	Due	
	Priority	
	Time	
Class:	Due	
	Priority	
	Time	
Class:	Due	
	Priority	
	Time	
Class:	Due	
	Priority	
	Time	
Class:	Due	
	Priority	
	Time	
Class:	Due	
	Priority	
	Time	

Heads up! Future due dates and tests:

What other commitments do I have today?

Where do I need help?

Work Plan

3:00
3:15
3:30
3:45
4:00
4:15
4:30
4:45
5:00
5:15
5:30
5:45
6:00
6:15
6:30
6:45
7:00
7:15
7:30
7:45
8:00
8:15
8:30
8:45
9:00
9:15
9:30
9:45
10:00
10:15
10:30
10:45

Three good things about me:

Friday, Date: _____

BULLETPROOF

Homework

Class:	Due	
	Priority	
	Time	
Class:	Due	
	Priority	
	Time	
Class:	Due	
	Priority	
	Time	
Class:	Due	
	Priority	
	Time	
Class:	Due	
	Priority	
	Time	
Class:	Due	
	Priority	
	Time	
Class:	Due	
	Priority	
	Time	

Heads up! Future due dates and tests:

What other commitments do I have today?

Where do I need help?

Work Plan

3:00
3:15
3:30
3:45
4:00
4:15
4:30
4:45
5:00
5:15
5:30
5:45
6:00
6:15
6:30
6:45
7:00
7:15
7:30
7:45
8:00
8:15
8:30
8:45
9:00
9:15
9:30
9:45
10:00
10:15
10:30
10:45

Three good things about me:

Saturday Plan
8:00
8:30
9:00
9:30
10:00
10:30
11:00
11:30
12:00
12:30
1:00
1:30
2:00
2:30
3:00
3:30
4:00
4:30
5:00
5:30
6:00
6:30
7:00
7:30
8:00
8:30
9:00
9:30
10:00
10:30

Sunday Plan
8:00
8:30
9:00
9:30
10:00
10:30
11:00
11:30
12:00
12:30
1:00
1:30
2:00
2:30
3:00
3:30
4:00
4:30
5:00
5:30
6:00
6:30
7:00
7:30
8:00
8:30
9:00
9:30
10:00
10:30

What worked this week? Or didn't?

My goals for next week:

Monday, Date: _____

BULLETPROOF

Homework

Class:		
	Due	
	Priority	
	Time	
Class:	Due	
	Priority	
	Time	
Class:	Due	
	Priority	
	Time	
Class:	Due	
	Priority	
	Time	
Class:	Due	
	Priority	
	Time	
Class:	Due	
	Priority	
	Time	
Class:	Due	
	Priority	
	Time	

Heads up! Future due dates and tests:

What other commitments do I have today?

Where do I need help?

Work Plan

3:00
3:15
3:30
3:45
4:00
4:15
4:30
4:45
5:00
5:15
5:30
5:45
6:00
6:15
6:30
6:45
7:00
7:15
7:30
7:45
8:00
8:15
8:30
8:45
9:00
9:15
9:30
9:45
10:00
10:15
10:30
10:45

Three good things about me:

Tuesday, Date: _____

Homework

Class:		Due	
		Priority	
		Time	
Class:		Due	
		Priority	
		Time	
Class:		Due	
		Priority	
		Time	
Class:		Due	
		Priority	
		Time	
Class:		Due	
		Priority	
		Time	
Class:		Due	
		Priority	
		Time	
Class:		Due	
		Priority	
		Time	

Heads up! Future due dates and tests:

What other commitments do I have today?

Where do I need help?

Work Plan

3:00
3:15
3:30
3:45
4:00
4:15
4:30
4:45
5:00
5:15
5:30
5:45
6:00
6:15
6:30
6:45
7:00
7:15
7:30
7:45
8:00
8:15
8:30
8:45
9:00
9:15
9:30
9:45
10:00
10:15
10:30
10:45

Three good things about me:

Wednesday, Date: _____

Homework

Class:	Due	
	Priority	
	Time	
Class:	Due	
	Priority	
	Time	
Class:	Due	
	Priority	
	Time	
Class:	Due	
	Priority	
	Time	
Class:	Due	
	Priority	
	Time	
Class:	Due	
	Priority	
	Time	
Class:	Due	
	Priority	
	Time	

Heads up! Future due dates and tests:

What other commitments do I have today?

Where do I need help?

Work Plan

3:00	
3:15	
3:30	
3:45	
4:00	
4:15	
4:30	
4:45	
5:00	
5:15	
5:30	
5:45	
6:00	
6:15	
6:30	
6:45	
7:00	
7:15	
7:30	
7:45	
8:00	
8:15	
8:30	
8:45	
9:00	
9:15	
9:30	
9:45	
10:00	
10:15	
10:30	
10:45	

Three good things about me:

Thursday, Date: _____

Homework

Class:	Due	
	Priority	
	Time	
Class:	Due	
	Priority	
	Time	
Class:	Due	
	Priority	
	Time	
Class:	Due	
	Priority	
	Time	
Class:	Due	
	Priority	
	Time	
Class:	Due	
	Priority	
	Time	
Class:	Due	
	Priority	
	Time	

Heads up! Future due dates and tests:

What other commitments do I have today?

Where do I need help?

Work Plan

3:00
3:15
3:30
3:45
4:00
4:15
4:30
4:45
5:00
5:15
5:30
5:45
6:00
6:15
6:30
6:45
7:00
7:15
7:30
7:45
8:00
8:15
8:30
8:45
9:00
9:15
9:30
9:45
10:00
10:15
10:30
10:45

Three good things about me:

Friday, Date: _____

BULLETPROOF

Homework

Class:			
		Due	
		Priority	
		Time	
Class:		Due	
		Priority	
		Time	
Class:		Due	
		Priority	
		Time	
Class:		Due	
		Priority	
		Time	
Class:		Due	
		Priority	
		Time	
Class:		Due	
		Priority	
		Time	
Class:		Due	
		Priority	
		Time	

Heads up! Future due dates and tests:

What other commitments do I have today?

Where do I need help?

Work Plan

Time	
3:00	
3:15	
3:30	
3:45	
4:00	
4:15	
4:30	
4:45	
5:00	
5:15	
5:30	
5:45	
6:00	
6:15	
6:30	
6:45	
7:00	
7:15	
7:30	
7:45	
8:00	
8:15	
8:30	
8:45	
9:00	
9:15	
9:30	
9:45	
10:00	
10:15	
10:30	
10:45	

Three good things about me:

BULLETPROOF

Saturday Plan	
8:00	
8:30	
9:00	
9:30	
10:00	
10:30	
11:00	
11:30	
12:00	
12:30	
1:00	
1:30	
2:00	
2:30	
3:00	
3:30	
4:00	
4:30	
5:00	
5:30	
6:00	
6:30	
7:00	
7:30	
8:00	
8:30	
9:00	
9:30	
10:00	
10:30	

Sunday Plan	
8:00	
8:30	
9:00	
9:30	
10:00	
10:30	
11:00	
11:30	
12:00	
12:30	
1:00	
1:30	
2:00	
2:30	
3:00	
3:30	
4:00	
4:30	
5:00	
5:30	
6:00	
6:30	
7:00	
7:30	
8:00	
8:30	
9:00	
9:30	
10:00	
10:30	

What worked this week? Or didn't?

My goals for next week:

Monday, Date: _____

Homework

Class:	Due	
	Priority	
	Time	
Class:	Due	
	Priority	
	Time	
Class:	Due	
	Priority	
	Time	
Class:	Due	
	Priority	
	Time	
Class:	Due	
	Priority	
	Time	
Class:	Due	
	Priority	
	Time	
Class:	Due	
	Priority	
	Time	

Heads up! Future due dates and tests:

What other commitments do I have today?

Where do I need help?

Work Plan

3:00
3:15
3:30
3:45
4:00
4:15
4:30
4:45
5:00
5:15
5:30
5:45
6:00
6:15
6:30
6:45
7:00
7:15
7:30
7:45
8:00
8:15
8:30
8:45
9:00
9:15
9:30
9:45
10:00
10:15
10:30
10:45

Three good things about me:

Tuesday, Date: _____

BULLETPROOF

Homework

Class:	Due	
	Priority	
	Time	
Class:	Due	
	Priority	
	Time	
Class:	Due	
	Priority	
	Time	
Class:	Due	
	Priority	
	Time	
Class:	Due	
	Priority	
	Time	
Class:	Due	
	Priority	
	Time	
Class:	Due	
	Priority	
	Time	

Heads up! Future due dates and tests:

What other commitments do I have today?

Where do I need help?

Work Plan

3:00
3:15
3:30
3:45
4:00
4:15
4:30
4:45
5:00
5:15
5:30
5:45
6:00
6:15
6:30
6:45
7:00
7:15
7:30
7:45
8:00
8:15
8:30
8:45
9:00
9:15
9:30
9:45
10:00
10:15
10:30
10:45

Three good things about me:

Wednesday, Date: _____

Homework

Class:	Due	
	Priority	
	Time	
Class:	Due	
	Priority	
	Time	
Class:	Due	
	Priority	
	Time	
Class:	Due	
	Priority	
	Time	
Class:	Due	
	Priority	
	Time	
Class:	Due	
	Priority	
	Time	
Class:	Due	
	Priority	
	Time	

Heads up! Future due dates and tests:

What other commitments do I have today?

Where do I need help?

Work Plan

3:00
3:15
3:30
3:45
4:00
4:15
4:30
4:45
5:00
5:15
5:30
5:45
6:00
6:15
6:30
6:45
7:00
7:15
7:30
7:45
8:00
8:15
8:30
8:45
9:00
9:15
9:30
9:45
10:00
10:15
10:30
10:45

Three good things about me:

Thursday, Date: _____

Homework

Class:	Due	
	Priority	
	Time	
Class:	Due	
	Priority	
	Time	
Class:	Due	
	Priority	
	Time	
Class:	Due	
	Priority	
	Time	
Class:	Due	
	Priority	
	Time	
Class:	Due	
	Priority	
	Time	
Class:	Due	
	Priority	
	Time	

Heads up! Future due dates and tests:

What other commitments do I have today?

Where do I need help?

Work Plan

3:00
3:15
3:30
3:45
4:00
4:15
4:30
4:45
5:00
5:15
5:30
5:45
6:00
6:15
6:30
6:45
7:00
7:15
7:30
7:45
8:00
8:15
8:30
8:45
9:00
9:15
9:30
9:45
10:00
10:15
10:30
10:45

Three good things about me:

Friday, Date: _____

Homework

Class:	Due	
	Priority	
	Time	
Class:	Due	
	Priority	
	Time	
Class:	Due	
	Priority	
	Time	
Class:	Due	
	Priority	
	Time	
Class:	Due	
	Priority	
	Time	
Class:	Due	
	Priority	
	Time	
Class:	Due	
	Priority	
	Time	

Heads up! Future due dates and tests:

What other commitments do I have today?

Where do I need help?

Work Plan

3:00
3:15
3:30
3:45
4:00
4:15
4:30
4:45
5:00
5:15
5:30
5:45
6:00
6:15
6:30
6:45
7:00
7:15
7:30
7:45
8:00
8:15
8:30
8:45
9:00
9:15
9:30
9:45
10:00
10:15
10:30
10:45

Three good things about me:

Saturday Plan

8:00	
8:30	
9:00	
9:30	
10:00	
10:30	
11:00	
11:30	
12:00	
12:30	
1:00	
1:30	
2:00	
2:30	
3:00	
3:30	
4:00	
4:30	
5:00	
5:30	
6:00	
6:30	
7:00	
7:30	
8:00	
8:30	
9:00	
9:30	
10:00	
10:30	

Sunday Plan

8:00	
8:30	
9:00	
9:30	
10:00	
10:30	
11:00	
11:30	
12:00	
12:30	
1:00	
1:30	
2:00	
2:30	
3:00	
3:30	
4:00	
4:30	
5:00	
5:30	
6:00	
6:30	
7:00	
7:30	
8:00	
8:30	
9:00	
9:30	
10:00	
10:30	

What worked this week? Or didn't?

My goals for next week:

Monday, Date: _____

Homework

Class:	Due	
	Priority	
	Time	
Class:	Due	
	Priority	
	Time	
Class:	Due	
	Priority	
	Time	
Class:	Due	
	Priority	
	Time	
Class:	Due	
	Priority	
	Time	
Class:	Due	
	Priority	
	Time	
Class:	Due	
	Priority	
	Time	

Heads up! Future due dates and tests:

What other commitments do I have today?

Where do I need help?

Work Plan

3:00
3:15
3:30
3:45
4:00
4:15
4:30
4:45
5:00
5:15
5:30
5:45
6:00
6:15
6:30
6:45
7:00
7:15
7:30
7:45
8:00
8:15
8:30
8:45
9:00
9:15
9:30
9:45
10:00
10:15
10:30
10:45

Three good things about me:

Tuesday, Date: _____

BULLETPROOF

Homework

Class:	Due	
	Priority	
	Time	
Class:	Due	
	Priority	
	Time	
Class:	Due	
	Priority	
	Time	
Class:	Due	
	Priority	
	Time	
Class:	Due	
	Priority	
	Time	
Class:	Due	
	Priority	
	Time	
Class:	Due	
	Priority	
	Time	

Heads up! Future due dates and tests:

What other commitments do I have today?

Where do I need help?

Work Plan

3:00
3:15
3:30
3:45
4:00
4:15
4:30
4:45
5:00
5:15
5:30
5:45
6:00
6:15
6:30
6:45
7:00
7:15
7:30
7:45
8:00
8:15
8:30
8:45
9:00
9:15
9:30
9:45
10:00
10:15
10:30
10:45

Three good things about me:

Wednesday, Date: _____

Homework

Class:	Due	
	Priority	
	Time	
Class:	Due	
	Priority	
	Time	
Class:	Due	
	Priority	
	Time	
Class:	Due	
	Priority	
	Time	
Class:	Due	
	Priority	
	Time	
Class:	Due	
	Priority	
	Time	
Class:	Due	
	Priority	
	Time	

Heads up! Future due dates and tests:

What other commitments do I have today?

Where do I need help?

Work Plan

3:00	
3:15	
3:30	
3:45	
4:00	
4:15	
4:30	
4:45	
5:00	
5:15	
5:30	
5:45	
6:00	
6:15	
6:30	
6:45	
7:00	
7:15	
7:30	
7:45	
8:00	
8:15	
8:30	
8:45	
9:00	
9:15	
9:30	
9:45	
10:00	
10:15	
10:30	
10:45	

Three good things about me:

Thursday, Date: _____

Homework

Class:	Due	
	Priority	
	Time	
Class:	Due	
	Priority	
	Time	
Class:	Due	
	Priority	
	Time	
Class:	Due	
	Priority	
	Time	
Class:	Due	
	Priority	
	Time	
Class:	Due	
	Priority	
	Time	
Class:	Due	
	Priority	
	Time	

Heads up! Future due dates and tests:

What other commitments do I have today?

Where do I need help?

Work Plan

3:00
3:15
3:30
3:45
4:00
4:15
4:30
4:45
5:00
5:15
5:30
5:45
6:00
6:15
6:30
6:45
7:00
7:15
7:30
7:45
8:00
8:15
8:30
8:45
9:00
9:15
9:30
9:45
10:00
10:15
10:30
10:45

Three good things about me:

Friday, Date: _____

BULLETPROOF

Homework

Class:	Due	
	Priority	
	Time	
Class:	Due	
	Priority	
	Time	
Class:	Due	
	Priority	
	Time	
Class:	Due	
	Priority	
	Time	
Class:	Due	
	Priority	
	Time	
Class:	Due	
	Priority	
	Time	
Class:	Due	
	Priority	
	Time	

Heads up! Future due dates and tests:

What other commitments do I have today?

Where do I need help?

Work Plan

3:00
3:15
3:30
3:45
4:00
4:15
4:30
4:45
5:00
5:15
5:30
5:45
6:00
6:15
6:30
6:45
7:00
7:15
7:30
7:45
8:00
8:15
8:30
8:45
9:00
9:15
9:30
9:45
10:00
10:15
10:30
10:45

Three good things about me:

BULLETPROOF

Saturday Plan
8:00
8:30
9:00
9:30
10:00
10:30
11:00
11:30
12:00
12:30
1:00
1:30
2:00
2:30
3:00
3:30
4:00
4:30
5:00
5:30
6:00
6:30
7:00
7:30
8:00
8:30
9:00
9:30
10:00
10:30

Sunday Plan
8:00
8:30
9:00
9:30
10:00
10:30
11:00
11:30
12:00
12:30
1:00
1:30
2:00
2:30
3:00
3:30
4:00
4:30
5:00
5:30
6:00
6:30
7:00
7:30
8:00
8:30
9:00
9:30
10:00
10:30

What worked this week? Or didn't?

My goals for next week:

Monday, Date: _____

BULLETPROOF

Homework

Class:		Due	
		Priority	
		Time	
Class:		Due	
		Priority	
		Time	
Class:		Due	
		Priority	
		Time	
Class:		Due	
		Priority	
		Time	
Class:		Due	
		Priority	
		Time	
Class:		Due	
		Priority	
		Time	
Class:		Due	
		Priority	
		Time	

Heads up! Future due dates and tests:

What other commitments do I have today?

Where do I need help?

Work Plan

3:00	
3:15	
3:30	
3:45	
4:00	
4:15	
4:30	
4:45	
5:00	
5:15	
5:30	
5:45	
6:00	
6:15	
6:30	
6:45	
7:00	
7:15	
7:30	
7:45	
8:00	
8:15	
8:30	
8:45	
9:00	
9:15	
9:30	
9:45	
10:00	
10:15	
10:30	
10:45	

Three good things about me:

Tuesday, Date: _____

BULLETPROOF

Homework

Class:			
	Due	
	Priority	
	Time	
Class:	Due	
	Priority	
	Time	
Class:	Due	
	Priority	
	Time	
Class:	Due	
	Priority	
	Time	
Class:	Due	
	Priority	
	Time	
Class:	Due	
	Priority	
	Time	
Class:	Due	
	Priority	
	Time	

Heads up! Future due dates and tests:

What other commitments do I have today?

Where do I need help?

Work Plan

3:00
3:15
3:30
3:45
4:00
4:15
4:30
4:45
5:00
5:15
5:30
5:45
6:00
6:15
6:30
6:45
7:00
7:15
7:30
7:45
8:00
8:15
8:30
8:45
9:00
9:15
9:30
9:45
10:00
10:15
10:30
10:45

Three good things about me:

Wednesday, Date: _____

Homework

Class:	Due	
	Priority	
	Time	
Class:	Due	
	Priority	
	Time	
Class:	Due	
	Priority	
	Time	
Class:	Due	
	Priority	
	Time	
Class:	Due	
	Priority	
	Time	
Class:	Due	
	Priority	
	Time	
Class:	Due	
	Priority	
	Time	

Heads up! Future due dates and tests:

What other commitments do I have today?

Where do I need help?

Work Plan

Time	
3:00	
3:15	
3:30	
3:45	
4:00	
4:15	
4:30	
4:45	
5:00	
5:15	
5:30	
5:45	
6:00	
6:15	
6:30	
6:45	
7:00	
7:15	
7:30	
7:45	
8:00	
8:15	
8:30	
8:45	
9:00	
9:15	
9:30	
9:45	
10:00	
10:15	
10:30	
10:45	

Three good things about me:

Thursday, Date: _____

Homework

Class:	Due	
	Priority	
	Time	
Class:	Due	
	Priority	
	Time	
Class:	Due	
	Priority	
	Time	
Class:	Due	
	Priority	
	Time	
Class:	Due	
	Priority	
	Time	
Class:	Due	
	Priority	
	Time	
Class:	Due	
	Priority	
	Time	

Heads up! Future due dates and tests:

What other commitments do I have today?

Where do I need help?

Work Plan

3:00
3:15
3:30
3:45
4:00
4:15
4:30
4:45
5:00
5:15
5:30
5:45
6:00
6:15
6:30
6:45
7:00
7:15
7:30
7:45
8:00
8:15
8:30
8:45
9:00
9:15
9:30
9:45
10:00
10:15
10:30
10:45

Three good things about me:

Friday, Date: _____

Homework

Class:		Due	
		Priority	
		Time	
Class:		Due	
		Priority	
		Time	
Class:		Due	
		Priority	
		Time	
Class:		Due	
		Priority	
		Time	
Class:		Due	
		Priority	
		Time	
Class:		Due	
		Priority	
		Time	
Class:		Due	
		Priority	
		Time	

Heads up! Future due dates and tests:

What other commitments do I have today?

Where do I need help?

Work Plan

3:00	
3:15	
3:30	
3:45	
4:00	
4:15	
4:30	
4:45	
5:00	
5:15	
5:30	
5:45	
6:00	
6:15	
6:30	
6:45	
7:00	
7:15	
7:30	
7:45	
8:00	
8:15	
8:30	
8:45	
9:00	
9:15	
9:30	
9:45	
10:00	
10:15	
10:30	
10:45	

Three good things about me:

BULLETPROOF

Saturday Plan	
8:00	
8:30	
9:00	
9:30	
10:00	
10:30	
11:00	
11:30	
12:00	
12:30	
1:00	
1:30	
2:00	
2:30	
3:00	
3:30	
4:00	
4:30	
5:00	
5:30	
6:00	
6:30	
7:00	
7:30	
8:00	
8:30	
9:00	
9:30	
10:00	
10:30	

Sunday Plan	
8:00	
8:30	
9:00	
9:30	
10:00	
10:30	
11:00	
11:30	
12:00	
12:30	
1:00	
1:30	
2:00	
2:30	
3:00	
3:30	
4:00	
4:30	
5:00	
5:30	
6:00	
6:30	
7:00	
7:30	
8:00	
8:30	
9:00	
9:30	
10:00	
10:30	

What worked this week? Or didn't?

My goals for next week:

Monday, Date: _____

Homework

Class:	Due	
	Priority	
	Time	
Class:	Due	
	Priority	
	Time	
Class:	Due	
	Priority	
	Time	
Class:	Due	
	Priority	
	Time	
Class:	Due	
	Priority	
	Time	
Class:	Due	
	Priority	
	Time	
Class:	Due	
	Priority	
	Time	

Heads up! Future due dates and tests:

What other commitments do I have today?

Where do I need help?

Work Plan

3:00
3:15
3:30
3:45
4:00
4:15
4:30
4:45
5:00
5:15
5:30
5:45
6:00
6:15
6:30
6:45
7:00
7:15
7:30
7:45
8:00
8:15
8:30
8:45
9:00
9:15
9:30
9:45
10:00
10:15
10:30
10:45

Three good things about me:

Tuesday, Date: _____

BULLETPROOF

Homework			
Class:	Due		
	Priority		
	Time		
Class:	Due		
	Priority		
	Time		
Class:	Due		
	Priority		
	Time		
Class:	Due		
	Priority		
	Time		
Class:	Due		
	Priority		
	Time		
Class:	Due		
	Priority		
	Time		
Class:	Due		
	Priority		
	Time		

Heads up! Future due dates and tests:

What other commitments do I have today?

Where do I need help?

Work Plan

3:00
3:15
3:30
3:45
4:00
4:15
4:30
4:45
5:00
5:15
5:30
5:45
6:00
6:15
6:30
6:45
7:00
7:15
7:30
7:45
8:00
8:15
8:30
8:45
9:00
9:15
9:30
9:45
10:00
10:15
10:30
10:45

Three good things about me:

Wednesday, Date: _____

Homework

Class:	Due	
	Priority	
	Time	
Class:	Due	
	Priority	
	Time	
Class:	Due	
	Priority	
	Time	
Class:	Due	
	Priority	
	Time	
Class:	Due	
	Priority	
	Time	
Class:	Due	
	Priority	
	Time	
Class:	Due	
	Priority	
	Time	

Heads up! Future due dates and tests:

What other commitments do I have today?

Where do I need help?

Work Plan

3:00
3:15
3:30
3:45
4:00
4:15
4:30
4:45
5:00
5:15
5:30
5:45
6:00
6:15
6:30
6:45
7:00
7:15
7:30
7:45
8:00
8:15
8:30
8:45
9:00
9:15
9:30
9:45
10:00
10:15
10:30
10:45

Three good things about me:

Thursday, Date: _____

Homework

Class:	Due	
	Priority	
	Time	
Class:	Due	
	Priority	
	Time	
Class:	Due	
	Priority	
	Time	
Class:	Due	
	Priority	
	Time	
Class:	Due	
	Priority	
	Time	
Class:	Due	
	Priority	
	Time	
Class:	Due	
	Priority	
	Time	

Heads up! Future due dates and tests:

What other commitments do I have today?

Where do I need help?

Work Plan

3:00
3:15
3:30
3:45
4:00
4:15
4:30
4:45
5:00
5:15
5:30
5:45
6:00
6:15
6:30
6:45
7:00
7:15
7:30
7:45
8:00
8:15
8:30
8:45
9:00
9:15
9:30
9:45
10:00
10:15
10:30
10:45

Three good things about me:

Friday, Date: _____

Homework

Class:	Due	
	Priority	
	Time	
Class:	Due	
	Priority	
	Time	
Class:	Due	
	Priority	
	Time	
Class:	Due	
	Priority	
	Time	
Class:	Due	
	Priority	
	Time	
Class:	Due	
	Priority	
	Time	
Class:	Due	
	Priority	
	Time	

Heads up! Future due dates and tests:

What other commitments do I have today?

Where do I need help?

Work Plan

3:00
3:15
3:30
3:45
4:00
4:15
4:30
4:45
5:00
5:15
5:30
5:45
6:00
6:15
6:30
6:45
7:00
7:15
7:30
7:45
8:00
8:15
8:30
8:45
9:00
9:15
9:30
9:45
10:00
10:15
10:30
10:45

Three good things about me:

BULLETPROOF

Saturday Plan	
8:00	
8:30	
9:00	
9:30	
10:00	
10:30	
11:00	
11:30	
12:00	
12:30	
1:00	
1:30	
2:00	
2:30	
3:00	
3:30	
4:00	
4:30	
5:00	
5:30	
6:00	
6:30	
7:00	
7:30	
8:00	
8:30	
9:00	
9:30	
10:00	
10:30	

Sunday Plan	
8:00	
8:30	
9:00	
9:30	
10:00	
10:30	
11:00	
11:30	
12:00	
12:30	
1:00	
1:30	
2:00	
2:30	
3:00	
3:30	
4:00	
4:30	
5:00	
5:30	
6:00	
6:30	
7:00	
7:30	
8:00	
8:30	
9:00	
9:30	
10:00	
10:30	

What worked this week? Or didn't?

My goals for next week:

Monday, Date: _____

BULLETPROOF

Homework

Class:	Due	
	Priority	
	Time	
Class:	Due	
	Priority	
	Time	
Class:	Due	
	Priority	
	Time	
Class:	Due	
	Priority	
	Time	
Class:	Due	
	Priority	
	Time	
Class:	Due	
	Priority	
	Time	
Class:	Due	
	Priority	
	Time	

Heads up! Future due dates and tests:

What other commitments do I have today?

Where do I need help?

Work Plan

3:00	
3:15	
3:30	
3:45	
4:00	
4:15	
4:30	
4:45	
5:00	
5:15	
5:30	
5:45	
6:00	
6:15	
6:30	
6:45	
7:00	
7:15	
7:30	
7:45	
8:00	
8:15	
8:30	
8:45	
9:00	
9:15	
9:30	
9:45	
10:00	
10:15	
10:30	
10:45	

Three good things about me:

Tuesday, Date: _____

BULLETPROOF

Homework

Class:		Due	
		Priority	
		Time	
Class:		Due	
		Priority	
		Time	
Class:		Due	
		Priority	
		Time	
Class:		Due	
		Priority	
		Time	
Class:		Due	
		Priority	
		Time	
Class:		Due	
		Priority	
		Time	
Class:		Due	
		Priority	
		Time	

Heads up! Future due dates and tests:

What other commitments do I have today?

Where do I need help?

Work Plan

3:00
3:15
3:30
3:45
4:00
4:15
4:30
4:45
5:00
5:15
5:30
5:45
6:00
6:15
6:30
6:45
7:00
7:15
7:30
7:45
8:00
8:15
8:30
8:45
9:00
9:15
9:30
9:45
10:00
10:15
10:30
10:45

Three good things about me:

Wednesday, Date: _____

Homework

Class:	Due	
	Priority	
	Time	
Class:	Due	
	Priority	
	Time	
Class:	Due	
	Priority	
	Time	
Class:	Due	
	Priority	
	Time	
Class:	Due	
	Priority	
	Time	
Class:	Due	
	Priority	
	Time	
Class:	Due	
	Priority	
	Time	

Heads up! Future due dates and tests:

What other commitments do I have today?

Where do I need help?

Work Plan

3:00
3:15
3:30
3:45
4:00
4:15
4:30
4:45
5:00
5:15
5:30
5:45
6:00
6:15
6:30
6:45
7:00
7:15
7:30
7:45
8:00
8:15
8:30
8:45
9:00
9:15
9:30
9:45
10:00
10:15
10:30
10:45

Three good things about me:

Thursday, Date: _____

Homework

Class:	Due	
	Priority	
	Time	
Class:	Due	
	Priority	
	Time	
Class:	Due	
	Priority	
	Time	
Class:	Due	
	Priority	
	Time	
Class:	Due	
	Priority	
	Time	
Class:	Due	
	Priority	
	Time	
Class:	Due	
	Priority	
	Time	

Heads up! Future due dates and tests:

What other commitments do I have today?

Where do I need help?

Work Plan

3:00
3:15
3:30
3:45
4:00
4:15
4:30
4:45
5:00
5:15
5:30
5:45
6:00
6:15
6:30
6:45
7:00
7:15
7:30
7:45
8:00
8:15
8:30
8:45
9:00
9:15
9:30
9:45
10:00
10:15
10:30
10:45

Three good things about me:

Friday, Date: _____

Homework

Class:	Due	
	Priority	
	Time	
Class:	Due	
	Priority	
	Time	
Class:	Due	
	Priority	
	Time	
Class:	Due	
	Priority	
	Time	
Class:	Due	
	Priority	
	Time	
Class:	Due	
	Priority	
	Time	
Class:	Due	
	Priority	
	Time	

Heads up! Future due dates and tests:

What other commitments do I have today?

Where do I need help?

Work Plan

3:00
3:15
3:30
3:45
4:00
4:15
4:30
4:45
5:00
5:15
5:30
5:45
6:00
6:15
6:30
6:45
7:00
7:15
7:30
7:45
8:00
8:15
8:30
8:45
9:00
9:15
9:30
9:45
10:00
10:15
10:30
10:45

Three good things about me:

BULLETPROOF

Saturday Plan	
8:00	
8:30	
9:00	
9:30	
10:00	
10:30	
11:00	
11:30	
12:00	
12:30	
1:00	
1:30	
2:00	
2:30	
3:00	
3:30	
4:00	
4:30	
5:00	
5:30	
6:00	
6:30	
7:00	
7:30	
8:00	
8:30	
9:00	
9:30	
10:00	
10:30	

Sunday Plan	
8:00	
8:30	
9:00	
9:30	
10:00	
10:30	
11:00	
11:30	
12:00	
12:30	
1:00	
1:30	
2:00	
2:30	
3:00	
3:30	
4:00	
4:30	
5:00	
5:30	
6:00	
6:30	
7:00	
7:30	
8:00	
8:30	
9:00	
9:30	
10:00	
10:30	

What worked this week? Or didn't?

My goals for next week:

Monday, Date: _____

Homework

Class:	Due	
	Priority	
	Time	
Class:	Due	
	Priority	
	Time	
Class:	Due	
	Priority	
	Time	
Class:	Due	
	Priority	
	Time	
Class:	Due	
	Priority	
	Time	
Class:	Due	
	Priority	
	Time	
Class:	Due	
	Priority	
	Time	

Heads up! Future due dates and tests:

What other commitments do I have today?

Where do I need help?

Work Plan

3:00
3:15
3:30
3:45
4:00
4:15
4:30
4:45
5:00
5:15
5:30
5:45
6:00
6:15
6:30
6:45
7:00
7:15
7:30
7:45
8:00
8:15
8:30
8:45
9:00
9:15
9:30
9:45
10:00
10:15
10:30
10:45

Three good things about me:

Tuesday, Date: _____

Homework

Class:	Due	
	Priority	
	Time	
Class:	Due	
	Priority	
	Time	
Class:	Due	
	Priority	
	Time	
Class:	Due	
	Priority	
	Time	
Class:	Due	
	Priority	
	Time	
Class:	Due	
	Priority	
	Time	
Class:	Due	
	Priority	
	Time	

Heads up! Future due dates and tests:

What other commitments do I have today?

Where do I need help?

Work Plan

Time	
3:00	
3:15	
3:30	
3:45	
4:00	
4:15	
4:30	
4:45	
5:00	
5:15	
5:30	
5:45	
6:00	
6:15	
6:30	
6:45	
7:00	
7:15	
7:30	
7:45	
8:00	
8:15	
8:30	
8:45	
9:00	
9:15	
9:30	
9:45	
10:00	
10:15	
10:30	
10:45	

Three good things about me:

Wednesday, Date: _____

BULLETPROOF

Homework

Class:		
	Due	
	Priority	
	Time	

Class:		
	Due	
	Priority	
	Time	

Class:		
	Due	
	Priority	
	Time	

Class:		
	Due	
	Priority	
	Time	

Class:		
	Due	
	Priority	
	Time	

Class:		
	Due	
	Priority	
	Time	

Class:		
	Due	
	Priority	
	Time	

Heads up! Future due dates and tests:

What other commitments do I have today?

Where do I need help?

Work Plan

3:00
3:15
3:30
3:45
4:00
4:15
4:30
4:45
5:00
5:15
5:30
5:45
6:00
6:15
6:30
6:45
7:00
7:15
7:30
7:45
8:00
8:15
8:30
8:45
9:00
9:15
9:30
9:45
10:00
10:15
10:30
10:45

Three good things about me:

Thursday, Date: _____

Homework

Class:	Due	
	Priority	
	Time	
Class:	Due	
	Priority	
	Time	
Class:	Due	
	Priority	
	Time	
Class:	Due	
	Priority	
	Time	
Class:	Due	
	Priority	
	Time	
Class:	Due	
	Priority	
	Time	
Class:	Due	
	Priority	
	Time	

Heads up! Future due dates and tests:

What other commitments do I have today?

Where do I need help?

Work Plan

3:00
3:15
3:30
3:45
4:00
4:15
4:30
4:45
5:00
5:15
5:30
5:45
6:00
6:15
6:30
6:45
7:00
7:15
7:30
7:45
8:00
8:15
8:30
8:45
9:00
9:15
9:30
9:45
10:00
10:15
10:30
10:45

Three good things about me:

Friday, Date: _____

Homework

Class:	Due	
	Priority	
	Time	
Class:	Due	
	Priority	
	Time	
Class:	Due	
	Priority	
	Time	
Class:	Due	
	Priority	
	Time	
Class:	Due	
	Priority	
	Time	
Class:	Due	
	Priority	
	Time	
Class:	Due	
	Priority	
	Time	

Heads up! Future due dates and tests:

What other commitments do I have today?

Where do I need help?

Work Plan

3:00
3:15
3:30
3:45
4:00
4:15
4:30
4:45
5:00
5:15
5:30
5:45
6:00
6:15
6:30
6:45
7:00
7:15
7:30
7:45
8:00
8:15
8:30
8:45
9:00
9:15
9:30
9:45
10:00
10:15
10:30
10:45

Three good things about me:

BULLETPROOF

Saturday Plan
8:00
8:30
9:00
9:30
10:00
10:30
11:00
11:30
12:00
12:30
1:00
1:30
2:00
2:30
3:00
3:30
4:00
4:30
5:00
5:30
6:00
6:30
7:00
7:30
8:00
8:30
9:00
9:30
10:00
10:30

Sunday Plan
8:00
8:30
9:00
9:30
10:00
10:30
11:00
11:30
12:00
12:30
1:00
1:30
2:00
2:30
3:00
3:30
4:00
4:30
5:00
5:30
6:00
6:30
7:00
7:30
8:00
8:30
9:00
9:30
10:00
10:30

What worked this week? Or didn't?

My goals for next week:

Monday, Date: _____

BULLETPROOF

Homework

Class:		Due	
		Priority	
		Time	
Class:		Due	
		Priority	
		Time	
Class:		Due	
		Priority	
		Time	
Class:		Due	
		Priority	
		Time	
Class:		Due	
		Priority	
		Time	
Class:		Due	
		Priority	
		Time	
Class:		Due	
		Priority	
		Time	

Heads up! Future due dates and tests:

What other commitments do I have today?

Where do I need help?

Work Plan

3:00	
3:15	
3:30	
3:45	
4:00	
4:15	
4:30	
4:45	
5:00	
5:15	
5:30	
5:45	
6:00	
6:15	
6:30	
6:45	
7:00	
7:15	
7:30	
7:45	
8:00	
8:15	
8:30	
8:45	
9:00	
9:15	
9:30	
9:45	
10:00	
10:15	
10:30	
10:45	

Three good things about me:

Tuesday, Date: _____

Homework

Class:		Due	
		Priority	
		Time	
Class:		Due	
		Priority	
		Time	
Class:		Due	
		Priority	
		Time	
Class:		Due	
		Priority	
		Time	
Class:		Due	
		Priority	
		Time	
Class:		Due	
		Priority	
		Time	
Class:		Due	
		Priority	
		Time	

Heads up! Future due dates and tests:

What other commitments do I have today?

Where do I need help?

Work Plan

3:00
3:15
3:30
3:45
4:00
4:15
4:30
4:45
5:00
5:15
5:30
5:45
6:00
6:15
6:30
6:45
7:00
7:15
7:30
7:45
8:00
8:15
8:30
8:45
9:00
9:15
9:30
9:45
10:00
10:15
10:30
10:45

Three good things about me:

Wednesday, Date: _____

BULLETPROOF

Homework

Class:		Due	
		Priority	
		Time	
Class:		Due	
		Priority	
		Time	
Class:		Due	
		Priority	
		Time	
Class:		Due	
		Priority	
		Time	
Class:		Due	
		Priority	
		Time	
Class:		Due	
		Priority	
		Time	
Class:		Due	
		Priority	
		Time	

Heads up! Future due dates and tests:

What other commitments do I have today?

Where do I need help?

Work Plan

3:00	
3:15	
3:30	
3:45	
4:00	
4:15	
4:30	
4:45	
5:00	
5:15	
5:30	
5:45	
6:00	
6:15	
6:30	
6:45	
7:00	
7:15	
7:30	
7:45	
8:00	
8:15	
8:30	
8:45	
9:00	
9:15	
9:30	
9:45	
10:00	
10:15	
10:30	
10:45	

Three good things about me:

Thursday, Date: _____

Homework

Class:		
	Due	
	Priority	
	Time	
Class:	Due	
	Priority	
	Time	
Class:	Due	
	Priority	
	Time	
Class:	Due	
	Priority	
	Time	
Class:	Due	
	Priority	
	Time	
Class:	Due	
	Priority	
	Time	
Class:	Due	
	Priority	
	Time	

Heads up! Future due dates and tests:

What other commitments do I have today?

Where do I need help?

Work Plan

3:00
3:15
3:30
3:45
4:00
4:15
4:30
4:45
5:00
5:15
5:30
5:45
6:00
6:15
6:30
6:45
7:00
7:15
7:30
7:45
8:00
8:15
8:30
8:45
9:00
9:15
9:30
9:45
10:00
10:15
10:30
10:45

Three good things about me:

Friday, Date: _____

Homework

Class:	Due	
	Priority	
	Time	
Class:	Due	
	Priority	
	Time	
Class:	Due	
	Priority	
	Time	
Class:	Due	
	Priority	
	Time	
Class:	Due	
	Priority	
	Time	
Class:	Due	
	Priority	
	Time	
Class:	Due	
	Priority	
	Time	

Heads up! Future due dates and tests:

What other commitments do I have today?

Where do I need help?

Work Plan

3:00	
3:15	
3:30	
3:45	
4:00	
4:15	
4:30	
4:45	
5:00	
5:15	
5:30	
5:45	
6:00	
6:15	
6:30	
6:45	
7:00	
7:15	
7:30	
7:45	
8:00	
8:15	
8:30	
8:45	
9:00	
9:15	
9:30	
9:45	
10:00	
10:15	
10:30	
10:45	

Three good things about me:

BULLETPROOF

Saturday Plan	
8:00	
8:30	
9:00	
9:30	
10:00	
10:30	
11:00	
11:30	
12:00	
12:30	
1:00	
1:30	
2:00	
2:30	
3:00	
3:30	
4:00	
4:30	
5:00	
5:30	
6:00	
6:30	
7:00	
7:30	
8:00	
8:30	
9:00	
9:30	
10:00	
10:30	

Sunday Plan	
8:00	
8:30	
9:00	
9:30	
10:00	
10:30	
11:00	
11:30	
12:00	
12:30	
1:00	
1:30	
2:00	
2:30	
3:00	
3:30	
4:00	
4:30	
5:00	
5:30	
6:00	
6:30	
7:00	
7:30	
8:00	
8:30	
9:00	
9:30	
10:00	
10:30	

What worked this week? Or didn't?

My goals for next week:

Monday, Date: _____

Homework

Class:	Due	
	Priority	
	Time	
Class:	Due	
	Priority	
	Time	
Class:	Due	
	Priority	
	Time	
Class:	Due	
	Priority	
	Time	
Class:	Due	
	Priority	
	Time	
Class:	Due	
	Priority	
	Time	
Class:	Due	
	Priority	
	Time	

Heads up! Future due dates and tests:

What other commitments do I have today?

Where do I need help?

Work Plan

3:00	
3:15	
3:30	
3:45	
4:00	
4:15	
4:30	
4:45	
5:00	
5:15	
5:30	
5:45	
6:00	
6:15	
6:30	
6:45	
7:00	
7:15	
7:30	
7:45	
8:00	
8:15	
8:30	
8:45	
9:00	
9:15	
9:30	
9:45	
10:00	
10:15	
10:30	
10:45	

Three good things about me:

Tuesday, Date: _____

BULLETPROOF

Homework

Class:	Due	
	Priority	
	Time	
Class:	Due	
	Priority	
	Time	
Class:	Due	
	Priority	
	Time	
Class:	Due	
	Priority	
	Time	
Class:	Due	
	Priority	
	Time	
Class:	Due	
	Priority	
	Time	
Class:	Due	
	Priority	
	Time	

Heads up! Future due dates and tests:

What other commitments do I have today?

Where do I need help?

Work Plan

3:00
3:15
3:30
3:45
4:00
4:15
4:30
4:45
5:00
5:15
5:30
5:45
6:00
6:15
6:30
6:45
7:00
7:15
7:30
7:45
8:00
8:15
8:30
8:45
9:00
9:15
9:30
9:45
10:00
10:15
10:30
10:45

Three good things about me:

Wednesday, Date: _____

Homework

Class:	Due	
	Priority	
	Time	
Class:	Due	
	Priority	
	Time	
Class:	Due	
	Priority	
	Time	
Class:	Due	
	Priority	
	Time	
Class:	Due	
	Priority	
	Time	
Class:	Due	
	Priority	
	Time	
Class:	Due	
	Priority	
	Time	

Heads up! Future due dates and tests:

What other commitments do I have today?

Where do I need help?

Work Plan

3:00
3:15
3:30
3:45
4:00
4:15
4:30
4:45
5:00
5:15
5:30
5:45
6:00
6:15
6:30
6:45
7:00
7:15
7:30
7:45
8:00
8:15
8:30
8:45
9:00
9:15
9:30
9:45
10:00
10:15
10:30
10:45

Three good things about me:

Thursday, Date: _____

Homework

Class:	Due	
	Priority	
	Time	
Class:	Due	
	Priority	
	Time	
Class:	Due	
	Priority	
	Time	
Class:	Due	
	Priority	
	Time	
Class:	Due	
	Priority	
	Time	
Class:	Due	
	Priority	
	Time	
Class:	Due	
	Priority	
	Time	

Heads up! Future due dates and tests:

What other commitments do I have today?

Where do I need help?

Work Plan

3:00
3:15
3:30
3:45
4:00
4:15
4:30
4:45
5:00
5:15
5:30
5:45
6:00
6:15
6:30
6:45
7:00
7:15
7:30
7:45
8:00
8:15
8:30
8:45
9:00
9:15
9:30
9:45
10:00
10:15
10:30
10:45

Three good things about me:

Friday, Date: _____

Homework

Class:	Due	
	Priority	
	Time	
Class:	Due	
	Priority	
	Time	
Class:	Due	
	Priority	
	Time	
Class:	Due	
	Priority	
	Time	
Class:	Due	
	Priority	
	Time	
Class:	Due	
	Priority	
	Time	
Class:	Due	
	Priority	
	Time	

Heads up! Future due dates and tests:

What other commitments do I have today?

Where do I need help?

Work Plan

3:00
3:15
3:30
3:45
4:00
4:15
4:30
4:45
5:00
5:15
5:30
5:45
6:00
6:15
6:30
6:45
7:00
7:15
7:30
7:45
8:00
8:15
8:30
8:45
9:00
9:15
9:30
9:45
10:00
10:15
10:30
10:45

Three good things about me:

BULLETPROOF

Saturday Plan
8:00
8:30
9:00
9:30
10:00
10:30
11:00
11:30
12:00
12:30
1:00
1:30
2:00
2:30
3:00
3:30
4:00
4:30
5:00
5:30
6:00
6:30
7:00
7:30
8:00
8:30
9:00
9:30
10:00
10:30

Sunday Plan
8:00
8:30
9:00
9:30
10:00
10:30
11:00
11:30
12:00
12:30
1:00
1:30
2:00
2:30
3:00
3:30
4:00
4:30
5:00
5:30
6:00
6:30
7:00
7:30
8:00
8:30
9:00
9:30
10:00
10:30

What worked this week? Or didn't?

My goals for next week:

Monday, Date: _____

Homework

Class:	Due	
	Priority	
	Time	
Class:	Due	
	Priority	
	Time	
Class:	Due	
	Priority	
	Time	
Class:	Due	
	Priority	
	Time	
Class:	Due	
	Priority	
	Time	
Class:	Due	
	Priority	
	Time	
Class:	Due	
	Priority	
	Time	

Heads up! Future due dates and tests:

What other commitments do I have today?

Where do I need help?

Work Plan

3:00	
3:15	
3:30	
3:45	
4:00	
4:15	
4:30	
4:45	
5:00	
5:15	
5:30	
5:45	
6:00	
6:15	
6:30	
6:45	
7:00	
7:15	
7:30	
7:45	
8:00	
8:15	
8:30	
8:45	
9:00	
9:15	
9:30	
9:45	
10:00	
10:15	
10:30	
10:45	

Three good things about me:

Tuesday, Date: _____

BULLETPROOF

Homework

Class:			
		Due	
		Priority	
		Time	
Class:		Due	
		Priority	
		Time	
Class:		Due	
		Priority	
		Time	
Class:		Due	
		Priority	
		Time	
Class:		Due	
		Priority	
		Time	
Class:		Due	
		Priority	
		Time	
Class:		Due	
		Priority	
		Time	

Heads up! Future due dates and tests:

What other commitments do I have today?

Where do I need help?

Work Plan

3:00
3:15
3:30
3:45
4:00
4:15
4:30
4:45
5:00
5:15
5:30
5:45
6:00
6:15
6:30
6:45
7:00
7:15
7:30
7:45
8:00
8:15
8:30
8:45
9:00
9:15
9:30
9:45
10:00
10:15
10:30
10:45

Three good things about me:

Wednesday, Date: _____

Homework

Class:	Due	
	Priority	
	Time	
Class:	Due	
	Priority	
	Time	
Class:	Due	
	Priority	
	Time	
Class:	Due	
	Priority	
	Time	
Class:	Due	
	Priority	
	Time	
Class:	Due	
	Priority	
	Time	
Class:	Due	
	Priority	
	Time	

Heads up! Future due dates and tests:

What other commitments do I have today?

Where do I need help?

Work Plan

3:00	
3:15	
3:30	
3:45	
4:00	
4:15	
4:30	
4:45	
5:00	
5:15	
5:30	
5:45	
6:00	
6:15	
6:30	
6:45	
7:00	
7:15	
7:30	
7:45	
8:00	
8:15	
8:30	
8:45	
9:00	
9:15	
9:30	
9:45	
10:00	
10:15	
10:30	
10:45	

Three good things about me:

Thursday, Date: _____

Homework

Class:	Due	
	Priority	
	Time	
Class:	Due	
	Priority	
	Time	
Class:	Due	
	Priority	
	Time	
Class:	Due	
	Priority	
	Time	
Class:	Due	
	Priority	
	Time	
Class:	Due	
	Priority	
	Time	
Class:	Due	
	Priority	
	Time	

Heads up! Future due dates and tests:

What other commitments do I have today?

Where do I need help?

Work Plan

3:00
3:15
3:30
3:45
4:00
4:15
4:30
4:45
5:00
5:15
5:30
5:45
6:00
6:15
6:30
6:45
7:00
7:15
7:30
7:45
8:00
8:15
8:30
8:45
9:00
9:15
9:30
9:45
10:00
10:15
10:30
10:45

Three good things about me:

Friday, Date: _____

Homework

Class:	Due	
	Priority	
	Time	
Class:	Due	
	Priority	
	Time	
Class:	Due	
	Priority	
	Time	
Class:	Due	
	Priority	
	Time	
Class:	Due	
	Priority	
	Time	
Class:	Due	
	Priority	
	Time	
Class:	Due	
	Priority	
	Time	

Heads up! Future due dates and tests:

What other commitments do I have today?

Where do I need help?

Work Plan

3:00
3:15
3:30
3:45
4:00
4:15
4:30
4:45
5:00
5:15
5:30
5:45
6:00
6:15
6:30
6:45
7:00
7:15
7:30
7:45
8:00
8:15
8:30
8:45
9:00
9:15
9:30
9:45
10:00
10:15
10:30
10:45

Three good things about me:

BULLETPROOF

Saturday Plan
8:00
8:30
9:00
9:30
10:00
10:30
11:00
11:30
12:00
12:30
1:00
1:30
2:00
2:30
3:00
3:30
4:00
4:30
5:00
5:30
6:00
6:30
7:00
7:30
8:00
8:30
9:00
9:30
10:00
10:30

Sunday Plan
8:00
8:30
9:00
9:30
10:00
10:30
11:00
11:30
12:00
12:30
1:00
1:30
2:00
2:30
3:00
3:30
4:00
4:30
5:00
5:30
6:00
6:30
7:00
7:30
8:00
8:30
9:00
9:30
10:00
10:30

What worked this week? Or didn't?

My goals for next week:

Monday, Date: _____

Homework

Class:	Due	
	Priority	
	Time	
Class:	Due	
	Priority	
	Time	
Class:	Due	
	Priority	
	Time	
Class:	Due	
	Priority	
	Time	
Class:	Due	
	Priority	
	Time	
Class:	Due	
	Priority	
	Time	
Class:	Due	
	Priority	
	Time	

Work Plan

3:00	
3:15	
3:30	
3:45	
4:00	
4:15	
4:30	
4:45	
5:00	
5:15	
5:30	
5:45	
6:00	
6:15	
6:30	
6:45	
7:00	
7:15	
7:30	
7:45	
8:00	
8:15	
8:30	
8:45	
9:00	
9:15	
9:30	
9:45	
10:00	
10:15	
10:30	
10:45	

Heads up! Future due dates and tests:

What other commitments do I have today?

Where do I need help?

Three good things about me:

Tuesday, Date: _____

BULLETPROOF

Homework

Class:	Due	
	Priority	
	Time	
Class:	Due	
	Priority	
	Time	
Class:	Due	
	Priority	
	Time	
Class:	Due	
	Priority	
	Time	
Class:	Due	
	Priority	
	Time	
Class:	Due	
	Priority	
	Time	
Class:	Due	
	Priority	
	Time	

Heads up! Future due dates and tests:

What other commitments do I have today?

Where do I need help?

Work Plan

3:00
3:15
3:30
3:45
4:00
4:15
4:30
4:45
5:00
5:15
5:30
5:45
6:00
6:15
6:30
6:45
7:00
7:15
7:30
7:45
8:00
8:15
8:30
8:45
9:00
9:15
9:30
9:45
10:00
10:15
10:30
10:45

Three good things about me:

Wednesday, Date: _____

BULLETPROOF

Homework

Class:	Due	
	Priority	
	Time	
Class:	Due	
	Priority	
	Time	
Class:	Due	
	Priority	
	Time	
Class:	Due	
	Priority	
	Time	
Class:	Due	
	Priority	
	Time	
Class:	Due	
	Priority	
	Time	
Class:	Due	
	Priority	
	Time	

Heads up! Future due dates and tests:

What other commitments do I have today?

Where do I need help?

Work Plan

| **3:00** |
| 3:15 |
| 3:30 |
| 3:45 |
| **4:00** |
| 4:15 |
| 4:30 |
| 4:45 |
| **5:00** |
| 5:15 |
| 5:30 |
| 5:45 |
| **6:00** |
| 6:15 |
| 6:30 |
| 6:45 |
| **7:00** |
| 7:15 |
| 7:30 |
| 7:45 |
| **8:00** |
| 8:15 |
| 8:30 |
| 8:45 |
| **9:00** |
| 9:15 |
| 9:30 |
| 9:45 |
| **10:00** |
| 10:15 |
| 10:30 |
| 10:45 |

Three good things about me:

Thursday, Date: _____

Homework

Class:	Due	
	Priority	
	Time	
Class:	Due	
	Priority	
	Time	
Class:	Due	
	Priority	
	Time	
Class:	Due	
	Priority	
	Time	
Class:	Due	
	Priority	
	Time	
Class:	Due	
	Priority	
	Time	
Class:	Due	
	Priority	
	Time	

Heads up! Future due dates and tests:

What other commitments do I have today?

Where do I need help?

Work Plan

3:00
3:15
3:30
3:45
4:00
4:15
4:30
4:45
5:00
5:15
5:30
5:45
6:00
6:15
6:30
6:45
7:00
7:15
7:30
7:45
8:00
8:15
8:30
8:45
9:00
9:15
9:30
9:45
10:00
10:15
10:30
10:45

Three good things about me:

Friday, Date: _____

BULLETPROOF

Homework

Class:	Due	
	Priority	
	Time	
Class:	Due	
	Priority	
	Time	
Class:	Due	
	Priority	
	Time	
Class:	Due	
	Priority	
	Time	
Class:	Due	
	Priority	
	Time	
Class:	Due	
	Priority	
	Time	
Class:	Due	
	Priority	
	Time	

Heads up! Future due dates and tests:

What other commitments do I have today?

Where do I need help?

Work Plan

3:00	
3:15	
3:30	
3:45	
4:00	
4:15	
4:30	
4:45	
5:00	
5:15	
5:30	
5:45	
6:00	
6:15	
6:30	
6:45	
7:00	
7:15	
7:30	
7:45	
8:00	
8:15	
8:30	
8:45	
9:00	
9:15	
9:30	
9:45	
10:00	
10:15	
10:30	
10:45	

Three good things about me:

Saturday Plan
8:00
8:30
9:00
9:30
10:00
10:30
11:00
11:30
12:00
12:30
1:00
1:30
2:00
2:30
3:00
3:30
4:00
4:30
5:00
5:30
6:00
6:30
7:00
7:30
8:00
8:30
9:00
9:30
10:00
10:30

Sunday Plan
8:00
8:30
9:00
9:30
10:00
10:30
11:00
11:30
12:00
12:30
1:00
1:30
2:00
2:30
3:00
3:30
4:00
4:30
5:00
5:30
6:00
6:30
7:00
7:30
8:00
8:30
9:00
9:30
10:00
10:30

What worked this week? Or didn't?

My goals for next week:

Made in the USA
Columbia, SC
08 December 2023

28027928R00093